ARBITRATION OF WAGES

PUBLICATIONS OF THE

INSTITUTE OF INDUSTRIAL RELATIONS

UNIVERSITY OF CALIFORNIA

ARBITRATION OF WAGES

By

IRVING BERNSTEIN

UNIVERSITY OF CALIFORNIA PRESS

BERKELEY AND LOS ANGELES

1954

331.2
B53

UNIVERSITY OF CALIFORNIA PRESS
BERKELEY AND LOS ANGELES
CALIFORNIA

◇

CAMBRIDGE UNIVERSITY PRESS
LONDON, ENGLAND

24329

LIBRARY OF CONGRESS CATALOG CARD NUMBER 54-10437
PRINTED IN THE UNITED STATES OF AMERICA
BY THE UNIVERSITY OF CALIFORNIA PRINTING DEPARTMENT

FOR

F. E. B.

FOREWORD

MOST CITIZENS would agree that labor-management disputes represent a vital area of study and analysis. In the light of this consideration, the Institute of Industrial Relations, Southern Division, has been conducting research into several aspects of this field for some time. The present volume, one of a group of related projects, seeks to assess the value of a key conflict-resolving mechanism, arbitration, on a critical conflict-provoking issue, wages.

The author's conclusion is that wage arbitration is neither a panacea nor a cipher; it may profitably be employed in some situations and not in others. With this statement and Mr. Bernstein's finding that "there is small risk in concluding that no more than 2 per cent of general wage changes in collective bargaining are arrived at through arbitration in peacetime," the casual reader might wonder about the value of a careful study such as is represented by this book. Actually, of course, wage arbitration is of much greater importance in the collective bargaining process than that figure indicates. It represents an important means for the peaceful settlement of differences in many dispute situations in which strikes might produce real hardships. More important, the decisions of arbitrators are widely used as guides by representatives of both management and labor in their negotiations, and the reasoning of these "third parties" often serves as a foundation for the thinking, as well as the argument, of the protagonists.

Since the end of World War II there has been much important research at various academic institutions dealing with the labor movement, collective bargaining, public policy, and dispute settlement. Although the primary influence of these studies has been on scholars and teachers, they have had an increasing impact in legislative chambers and at the bargaining table. Mr. Bernstein's writings represent a significant part of the worth-while research in these areas. Although he was trained as a historian, his studies are constantly alive to the importance of current attitudes and activities, such as those discussed in this book. The Institute takes pride in presenting this volume on the *Arbitration of Wages*.

EDGAR L. WARREN, *Director*
Southern Division
Los Angeles, California

PREFACE

THIS STUDY of arbitration revolves about the unifying problem of the general wage change, certainly one of the critical issues of collective bargaining. It has several objectives. The first is to examine the institutional situations in which wage arbitration functions. The second is to offer comment on those procedural questions that are peculiar to the arbitration of this issue. Finally, and perhaps most important, the monograph codifies and analyzes the disposition of the criteria of wage determination under the unusually favorable circumstances that arbitration affords.

With respect to method, primary reliance has been placed upon the cases themselves, which reveal, in Feis's words, "the broken surfaces of economic life that must be sewed together again. . . ."[1] This is not to say that the literature on arbitration has been ignored; it has, in fact, been examined carefully. The cases, however, receive first emphasis because the study is more concerned with disputes than it is with wage concepts, even when the latter are discussed.

The Bureau of National Affairs, *Labor Arbitration Reports,* makes the most complete set of awards available to research workers with a minimum expenditure of effort. The footnote citation, *LA,* refers to this series. Several sections of the monograph are based upon all the published awards of general wage changes from the inception of the *Reports,* 1945, to the outbreak of the Korean War in midyear, 1950. Decisions since the latter date are not systematically included because they reflect unusual economic and institutional considerations that shed little light on peacetime wage arbitration. The more recent awards, however, have been used occasionally as dictated by their individual relevance to the study.

Of necessity, sole reliance has been placed upon the award as written; it is simply not workable to look behind the printed page. In light of that fact, no one experienced in collective bargaining and arbitration can be fully satisfied, for he must recognize that what remains unsaid may be decisive. Efforts made to probe the vital and elusive area of motive are based on sources other than the published awards.

The fact that this study codifies wage decisions necessitates a word of caution. Unions, employers, and arbitrators may find it a convenient source for those principles that have been evolved. Many issues, however, remain in dispute. Hence this volume is not intended to be the

---

[1] Herbert Feis, *Principles of Wage Settlement* (New York: Wilson, 1924), p. 3.

arbitrator's "handy guide." There is no final word in an area as fluid as industrial relations.

The organization of the material dealing with the criteria of wage determination presents a problem that the reader, unfortunately, must share. Chapters iv and v deal with them in approximately descending order of importance. To ease finding the discussion of a particular factor, the table of contents sets forth the breakdown of these chapters in detail.

A factor which does not lend itself to systematic analysis is the role of the arbitrator's judgment in performing his function. Here the qualities called for are perhaps best illustrated by recounting Carl Sandburg's children's tale from the *Rootabaga Stories*.

One winter it was so cold that all the animals' tails were frozen and blown away by a big wind. The rabbits did not mind because they had so little to lose. The flongboos, however, were disturbed because their tails were long and were fitted with electric lights to illuminate their houses. They decided to do something and appointed a "Committee of 66."

The Committee of 66 had a meeting and a parleyhoo to decide what steps could be taken by talking to do something. For chairman they picked an old flongboo who was an umpire and used to umpire many mix-ups. Among the flongboos he was called "the umpire of umpires," "the king of umpires," "the prince of umpires," "the peer of umpires." When there was a fight and a snag and a wrangle between two families living next door neighbors to each other, and this old flongboo was called in to umpire and to say which family started it and which family ought to stop it, he used to say, "The best umpire is the one who knows just how far to go and how far not to go."[2]

The Institute's reading committee, consisting of Paul A. Dodd, J. A. C. Grant, and J. Fred Weston, offered many valuable suggestions. The volume has also benefited from the careful reading and friendly criticism of Benjamin Aaron, Clark Kerr, Frank C. Pierson, Arthur M. Ross, and Edgar L. Warren. Mrs. Anne P. Cook performed the editorial work and prepared the index. Mrs. Lois Hurwitz typed the manuscript. Several publishers have granted permission to quote from their works: Ronald Press for Z. Clark Dickinson, *Collective Wage Determination,* University of Pennsylvania Press for Thomas Kennedy, *Effective Labor Arbitration,* and Harcourt, Brace for Carl Sandburg, *Rootabaga Stories.* To these individuals and publishers I wish to express deep gratitude. Needless to say, they share no responsibility for errors of fact or for the viewpoint expressed.

IRVING BERNSTEIN

---

[2] Carl Sandburg, *Rootabaga Stories* (New York: Harcourt, Brace, 1922), pp. 218–219.

CONTENTS

Tables

Figures

I. INTRODUCTION

THE PURPOSE of this introductory chapter is to erect a framework about which walls may later be hung. It seeks to accomplish this objective in two ways, first, by sketching roughly the historic development of wage arbitration in this country and, second, by fitting this procedure into the broader patterns of collective bargaining and wage determination.

1. A Brief History of Wage Arbitration

The systematic gathering of arbitration awards in the United States is, unfortunately, of recent origin. Hence one is prevented from recording in some detail the utilization of this procedure in wage disputes. The evidence at hand, however, does permit a rough sketch of development and suggests the origin of important characteristics of wage arbitration as now practiced.

The first case of certain record occurred in 1871. Judge William Elwell, of Bloomsburg, Pennsylvania, decided a wage dispute between the Committee of the Anthracite Board of Trade and the Committee of the Workingmen's Benevolent Association. It was followed three years later by another coal wage arbitration in Ohio. Between that time and the onset of World War I, unions and employers enlarged their use of this procedure, but at a slow pace. The Bureau of Labor Statistics, in fact, uncovered no more than fifty-four awards in wage cases for the half century following the Civil War. They broke down by industry groups into twenty-eight industrial (manufacturing?), twenty-two railway, and four urban transit cases.[1]

Government sought to encourage the development of voluntary arbitration in this period. At the federal level, this encouragement was confined to the railways and reflected deep public disturbance over grievous railroad strikes. The Arbitration Act of 1888, the Erdman Act of 1898, and the Newlands Act of 1913 emerged from this concern. Under the last two of these laws, carriers and railway unions arbitrated twenty general wage changes before the middle of 1914, as well as two disputes outside the statutory system. Similarly, in the last two decades of the nineteenth century no fewer than seventeen states created arbitration agencies to deal with disputes in industry generally. These boards, however, were seldom called into service.[2]

---

[1] Edwin E. Witte, *Historical Survey of Labor Arbitration*, Labor Relations Series (Philadelphia: University of Pennsylvania Press, 1952), p. 11; "Results of Arbitration Cases Involving Wages and Hours, 1865–1929," *Monthly Labor Review*, XXIX (November, 1929), 16.

[2] J. Noble Stockett, Jr., *The Arbitral Determination of Railway Wages* (Boston: Houghton Mifflin, 1918), pp. xxiii–xxiv; Edwin E. Witte, "The Future of Labor Arbitration—A Challenge," First Annual Meeting of the National Academy of Arbitrators, Chicago, January 16, 1948, p. 9.

In the period before 1914, employers and unions in some industries privately agreed to wage arbitration with some regularity. The American Newspaper Publishers Association and the printing trades, for example, created a continuing contract arbitration arrangement in 1901. Between 1902 and 1907 the United Typothetae and the Printing Pressmen adopted this scheme in their segment of the book and job branch of the industry. In New York, at least, all the unions in this phase of printing accepted a similar plan in the years 1907–1913. The shoe industry in Massachusetts witnessed its first wage award in 1885, and employed the process from time to time thereafter. Perhaps the most important wage decision of the time was that granted by the Anthracite Coal Commission following the great strike of 1902.[3]

Wage arbitration grew phenomenally during the era of World War I. As contrasted with the fifty-four awards in the prior half century, the BLS reported 423 for 1915–1920, excluding 2,000 by wartime government agencies. Many industries employed the process, and it is probable that transit began its general use at this time. The same expansion was evident in the New York City book and job printing industry—twenty-three private wage cases between 1917 and 1922. The climax was reached in 1920 when this procedure was used to determine industry-wide wage changes in bituminous and anthracite coal and on the railroads.[4]

At the same time, government intervened on a wide scale to fix wages with arbitration, notably through the National War Labor Board. The Transportation Act of 1920 created the U. S. Railroad Labor Board, with authority to determine wage rates for railway employees in accordance with a generally stated set of statutory criteria. In the same year, Kansas prohibited strikes in key industries and established an Industrial Court to resolve disputes, in the case of wages according to standards patterned after those of the Transportation Act.

The reasons for this mushrooming of wage arbitration are not hard to find. The period witnessed extraordinary changes in the price level. The BLS Cost of Living Index, for example, shot upward from 71.8 in 1914 (1935–1939 = 100) to 143.3 in 1920, and then declined sharply to 119.7 in 1922. This factor joined with wartime full employment and an encouraging government policy to foster the rapid spread of union-

[3] James F. Bogardus, *Industrial Arbitration in the Book and Job Printing Industry of New York City* (Philadelphia: University of Pennsylvania Press, 1934), pp. 32, 40; Thomas L. Norton, *Trade-Union Policies in the Massachusetts Shoe Industry, 1919–1929* (New York: Columbia University Press, 1932), pp. 351–352; Elma B. Carr, *The Use of Cost-of-Living Figures in Wage Adjustments,* Bureau of Labor Statistics, Bull. no. 369 (Washington: 1923), pp. 7–10.

[4] "Results of Arbitration Cases," *op. cit.,* pp. 14–15, 18; Bogardus, *op. cit.,* p. 98.

ism. Since many unions were weak or otherwise reluctant to strike, they were eager to arbitrate wage changes. In the inflationary phase of the period the key criterion was cost of living; in fact, it entered into virtually all the awards. The other influential factor was the living wage, that is, the minimum necessary to maintain a given standard of life. It received particular attention at the hands of NWLB and in the great mining and railway cases of 1920.[5]

In face of the deflation of 1920–1922, unions were more reluctant to entrust wage determination to third parties, and the number of awards dropped off, though remaining high as contrasted with the prewar level. In this period, perhaps for the first time, some labor organizations and employers turned to wage arbitration as a device for administering least painfully a wage cut that both recognized as necessary. As prices came down and unemployment spread, the standards changed: the financial condition of the employer became crucial and employers turned the cost-of-living argument against employees. Unions countered with the living-wage, productivity, and consumer-purchasing-power arguments.[6]

The record for the period between 1922 and World War II permits no more than a general outline. The paramount fact, of which there is no doubt, is that wage arbitration declined sharply in the 'twenties. At this time, for example, the United Mine Workers, reversing earlier practice, declared themselves vigorously opposed to the process. Conditions after 1920 were hardly ripe: unions were fighting a hapless rearguard action against postwar depression and the "American Plan," while the cost of living was relatively stable. In this decade, wage arbitration was common only in urban transit and was used sparingly in printing, men's garments, the electrical trades, and the Massachusetts shoe industry.[7] The governmental systems erected in the previous era suffered a similar decline. The wartime agencies, of course, disappeared with the end of hostilities. The Railway Labor Act of 1926 junked the Railroad Labor Board and stripped its successor of the power to fix wages. The Kansas statute failed to survive court review on constitutional grounds.

The growth of collective bargaining accompanying the revival of business conditions and prices in the New Deal period undoubtedly led to some upturn in the utilization of wage arbitration. It probably did

---

[5] Carr, *op. cit.*, p. 431; M. L. Stecker, "Family Budgets and Wages," *American Economic Review*, XI (September, 1921), 448–450.
[6] George Soule, *Wage Arbitration, Selected Cases, 1920–1924* (New York: Macmillan, 1928), pp. 9–10.
[7] "Results of Arbitration Cases," *op. cit.*, p. 19; Norton, *op. cit., passim.*

not reach the level of 1914–1922.[8] World War II and the postwar inflation paralleled the experience of World War I. Rapid price changes,
full employment, and a great expansion of collective bargaining provided a fertile soil for wage arbitration. The second National War
Labor Board and related agencies disposed of thousands of wage cases
during the war, while a number of states after V-J Day created compulsory arbitration bodies to decide wage controversies in public
utilities. After the war, private wage arbitration won widespread favor,
the particular nature of which will be the burden of later sections of
this study.

This sketchy history suggests several generalizations: Wage arbitration, quite clearly, has not been accepted generally or permanently in
American industry. Although its use has grown since the Civil War,
the expansion has come in spurts rather than continuously. At times of
sharp price change, particularly during and after great wars, unions
and management have employed private wage arbitration as a frequent
substitute for collective bargaining. In such periods, government, both
federal and state, has encouraged or required its use. When prices have
been stable, on the other hand, this procedure has won little favor. A
few industries, notably urban transit, printing, garments, shoes, and (in
some periods) railroads, have tended to engage in wage arbitration
with some regularity over a fairly long period of time.

These generalizations suggest the need to establish at this point
several fundamental characteristics of the arbitration of wages that precondition an understanding of what is to follow.

2. *Certain Underlying Considerations*

A realistic comprehension of wage arbitration must rest upon three
basic considerations: first, that this process is a function of collective
bargaining as practiced in the United States; second, that it is shaped
by the patterns of union and management behavior; and, finally, that
generally accepted standards of wage determination, eminently desirable though they would be, do not exist.

Arbitrators with a penchant for turning a well-worn phrase seldom
fail to observe in wage awards that contract arbitration is an "extension" of or "substitute" for collective bargaining. The literature is heavy
with restatements of this notion. An old coin, however, is worth no less
than a new one.

---

[8] Disputes submitted to the New York Mediation Board for arbitration (including
nonwage matters) following its establishment in 1937 reinforce this conclusion. *Report
of the New York State Joint Legislative Committee on Industrial and Labor Conditions,* Legis. Doc. no. 50 (Albany: 1944), p. 31.

This concept, in theory at least, distinguishes contract arbitration on the one hand from grievance arbitration and the judicial process on the other. The grievance umpire is presumed to have his feet planted firmly on the jointly negotiated agreement, and the judge operates from the secure base of the statute or the common law. The contract arbitrator, by contrast, must venture alone into the unknown without guideposts. This dichotomy, though useful for purposes of analysis, only half describes the real world. Agreement writing being what it is, grievance arbitrators spend much time divining what the parties would have accepted to cover a point on which the contract is silent or resolving a conflict between several of its sections. Judges encounter related difficulties. By the same token, the parties restrict the authority of wage arbitrators with submission agreements and arbitrators themselves reveal a reluctant venturesomeness by the standards they emphasize, notably comparisons.

Within these limits, nevertheless, the distinction is valid. Its soundness is readily apparent from a consideration of the potential range of decision-making. The judge (and the grievance arbitrator) must take three factors into account: the positions of the two disputants and the law (or the agreement). It is entirely possible that the law (or the agreement) does not coincide with the demand of either party, and, in that eventuality, he is under compulsion to render a decision that pleases neither litigant. In wage arbitration, by contrast, the range is fixed within the limits of the positions of the parties. If the union asks ten cents and the employer offers five, the arbitrator invites disaster by awarding less than five or more than ten, regardless of logic or equity. Those who doubt may study with profit the notorious Landis award of 1921 in the Chicago building industry.[9]

Emerging as it does out of collective bargaining, wage arbitration operates on the same bases and is bounded by the same limitations. Bargaining rests ultimately, of course, upon the right of union or management to withdraw labor or jobs. The collective agreement is a sign that they have elected peace rather than war for the duration of its term. If they choose to arbitrate, or, in Soule's phrase, take "the peaceful uncertainty of an arbitral settlement," they have implicitly agreed that it is preferable to the costs and risks of a strike or lockout. Sophisticated parties expect, and properly so, that the neutral's decision will approximate what they would voluntarily have agreed upon themselves. Hence he is obliged to consider not only the general standards of wage determination but also the parties' relative bargaining

[9] See below, pp. 41–42.

power. If he fails to do so, he may well undermine his basic function—keeping the peace.[10]

This leads directly to a second basic relationship of bargaining to arbitration, namely, acceptability. A rejected decision is no decision at all. Hence the arbitrator must recognize that his ruling is "useless if it cannot be enforced, and that the power and ability of the respective parties to administer a decision successfully is an integral part of the decision itself."[11] Again, he will have betrayed his purpose if his award produces a work stoppage.

In this light there is pressure upon the arbitrator to give weight to those standards of wage determination which the parties themselves would have emphasized in bargaining and to disregard those that they would have ignored. As a result, his award is a product of mixed considerations: the economic and the political, the measurable and the immeasurable, the rational and the inconsistent. "A wage arbitration," Soule has noted, "is not an exercise in pure reason."[12] When the parties have given the arbitrator no guidance as to the criteria they wish him to apply, his safest policy is to accept what has been decided in collective bargaining in a competing or related firm. This suggests, Kerr has pointed out, "how experienced bargainers have evaluated the wage influencing factors which have evidenced themselves, and what they consider to be 'just.' . . . The 'pattern' . . . indicates what might have evolved from successful bargaining had the parties acted like others similarly situated."[13] It also helps to explain the unusual weight which arbitrators lend to comparisons in reaching their decisions.

This analysis suggests that the arbitrator's written opinion does not necessarily reveal the process by which he reaches his decision. There is, however, an occasional award that reveals the full impact of bargaining, and such an exception merits quoting at length.

> The Board has applied no *a priori* principles of wage determination to the welter of evidence and argument developed by the parties. It accepts with some discrimination of values the several pertinent criteria emphasized by one side and the other. Candor requires it to be said, however, that the Board, in deliberation, advanced

---

[10] David L. Cole, for example, has said of the street railway organization: "A Union which in its constitution forbids strikes in favor of arbitration assuredly should not be held to lesser benefits by arbitrators than they would have attained by more conventional processes." Atlantic City Transportation Co. and Amalgamated Street Railway Employees, 9 *LA* 578 (1948). See also Capital Transit Co. and Amalgamated Street Railway Employees, 9 *LA* 666 (1947). A board reached the same conclusion in the face of a state statute denying the employees of a public utility the right to strike. Dairyland Power Coop. and Brotherhood of Electrical Workers, 14 *LA* 737 (1950).

[11] Soule, *op. cit.*, pp. 6–7.

[12] *Loc. cit.*

[13] Pacific Gas & Electric Co. and Utility Workers, 7 *LA* 534 (1947). See also Durso & Geelan Co. and Teamsters, 17 *LA* 748 (1951).

its thinking at once to an area within the narrow limits to which direct collective bargaining, as made known on the record, had brought the parties when dead-locked. Pragmatically, absent certitude or fiat in such matters, "principles" forged by the parties themselves are fair guides, in labor relations especially, to solutions designed to achieve mutual acceptance if not cold intellectual satisfaction. Thus we brushed aside the one-time 25-cent figure the union doubtless had not seriously meant to get and the 16 cents it probably did not expect to get; we did not dwell on the zero or 7-cent suggestions with which the company tilted. We proceeded to find, as the parties by their aborted bargaining had acknowledged, that some increase in the neighborhood of 8 to 11 cents was probably justified by a fair and equitable accommodation of all governing principles. The precise amount and the application of any given increase were the posers.[14]

Considered as a phase of collective bargaining, wage arbitration comes into focus as a tactic of unions and management in achieving their strategic objectives in bargaining. This necessitates a summary examination of the parties' goals in wage negotiations.

There is constant pressure upon the union to raise the wages—money and real—of its members. As James O'Connell, president of the AFL Metal Trades Department, declared in 1917, "I hope the Boilermakers in convention here will get in their minds that beautiful thought of 'more.'"[15] Workers are continuously anxious to enlarge their incomes and to maintain or expand their share of a rising national product. "This is a one-way street—precisely as technical and economic progress is a one-way development."[16] This economic urge is reinforced by institutional considerations. The rank and file tends to measure the effectiveness of its leadership in large part with the yardstick of "delivering" on wages. The worker is persuaded by a higher wage rate that the leaders deserve to remain in office and that the union is entitled to support. The other side of this coin is the virtual unanimity of workers and unions in opposition to wage-cutting regardless of circumstances. In the great railway shopmen's strike of 1922, for example, the unions maintained a hopeless struggle in the face of certain defeat because the leaders recognized that the men would not voluntarily accept a wage reduction.[17]

This constant striving for "more" (and resistance to "less"), though suggesting a direction, reveals little about how unions formulate wage policies. "It is hard to give any general answer to this question, because union leaders do not follow fixed policies or standards. Their

[14] Public Service Electric & Gas Co. and Chemical Workers, 12 *LA* 671 (1949).

[15] Quoted in V. W. Lanfear, *Business Fluctuations in the American Labor Movement* (New York: Columbia University Press, 1924), p. 88.

[16] W. S. Woytinsky and Associates, *Labor and Management Look at Collective Bargaining* (New York: Twentieth Century Fund, 1949), p. xxvi.

[17] H. D. Wolf, *The Railroad Labor Board* (Chicago: University of Chicago Press, 1927), p. 263.

thinking, like that of businessmen, is pragmatic rather than theoretical."[18] Reynolds suggests that the considerations to which they lend greatest weight are these: (1) rank-and-file sentiment, (2) wage increases recently won by other unions, (3) the economic condition of the industry, and (4) nonunion competition in the industry, where it exists. The precise amount that a union will ask for and/or insist upon, of course, cannot be generalized. It represents a balance of these considerations and perhaps others in a particular context.

The twin forces working within the union—economic and institutional—exert pressure for higher money wages regardless of the effect upon real wages. "The average man," a management spokesman has observed, "likes to handle money. He'd probably prefer to have $60 a week and inflation which eats it all up rather than $40 a week that allows him to live and save a little."[19] This rank-and-file attitude is joined by the union's need to demonstrate its effectiveness to its members. The individual labor organization can hardly assume responsibility for a general decline in the price level, but it can claim full credit for a particular wage increase. In fact, it does not directly fix prices at all. Hence the argument that a wage demand in a given set of negotiations will be inflationary is not likely to impress either the worker or the leader. Similarly, unions tend to discount the employment effect of a wage adjustment. They will not, with some exceptions, accept a lower wage in the hope that it will result in higher employment.[20]

The policies of management toward general wage changes reflect the same forces, economic and institutional, that motivate unions, but the institutional are of less importance. This, in part, is because the employer is primarily concerned with the economic health of his own firm, whereas the union's policies are geared to the several companies with which it deals. In addition, management is typically more secure than union leadership and is therefore under less pressure to demonstrate effectiveness to its constituents. Institutional considerations gain in significance on the management side when bargaining is conducted through an employers' association or, in the case of a small concern, in an industry dominated by a large one. An association, for example, may shape a wage policy with an eye to its own survival.

A company is prepared to offer a wage, Reynolds points out, that is between "the maximum which it can afford to pay and the minimum

---

[18] Lloyd G. Reynolds, *Labor Economics and Labor Relations* (New York: Prentice-Hall, 1949), p. 379.

[19] Quoted in Woytinsky, *op. cit.*, p. 86.

[20] For a discussion of this point, see Arthur M. Ross, *Trade Union Wage Policy* (Berkeley: University of California Press, 1948), pp. 78–80.

necessary to recruit workers in the local labor market."[21] This definition is convenient but hardly precise. The range may be very wide, and each extremity is a variable. Finally, these factors fluctuate over time. To take an extreme example: An employer to whom labor cost is a minor element in total cost may be able to pay approximately $3.00 per hour for a given grade of labor, while it may be available for about $1.00. If he had to pay $3.50 to get it, he might institute economies in the non-labor segments of his operations or raise his product price, depending upon the state of the market. At the other end, he might recruit a more desirable labor force at $1.50. His choice of alternatives, clearly, is very wide.

In fixing a wage within this range, employers tend to lend greatest weight to these factors: (1) the financial condition of the firm and the industry, (2) the wage rates and general adjustments offered by other employers in the industry, (3) the wage rates paid by other firms in the local labor market, (4) patterns established in other industries, and (5) the general strategy toward the union, for example, to weaken or strengthen the faction in power. Again, the precise amount cannot be generalized since it is the product of a balancing of these factors in a specific context.

The thread that runs through both union and management behavior is comparability, or, as Ross has phrased it, the "equitable comparison." This factor is vital to the worker because it is a basic yardstick for determining the acceptability of his wage. Comparisons are equally important to the union as the means of demonstrating its effectiveness, particularly under conditions of rival unionism. The employer is, as well, motivated by comparability in order to stay in step with his competitors and the business community at large. Ross observes, "the employer can believe that he has not given away too much, and the union leader that he has achieved enough."[22] Finally, arbitrators, as will be noted in detail later, are no less reliant upon comparisons than the parties in making up their minds.

The wage arbitration policies of unions and management fit into this pattern of their behavior in negotiations. For both the labor organization and the employer the wage is the end; the device by which it is attained is the means. In their view, accordingly, voluntary wage arbitration is subordinate to the wage agreement they seek to achieve. They employ it opportunistically, that is, in those situations in which they calculate that their wage goals cannot be reached in another manner.

It has often been observed that the decision to employ this procedure

---

[21] Reynolds, *op. cit.*, p. 377.
[22] Ross, *op. cit.*, p. 52.

is inherently a sign of weakness. For the union it is an alternative to the strike, and the organization that possesses economic power and is prepared to use it does not normally arbitrate. "There's no way," a union spokesman has declared, "of using the power of an organization on an arbitrator."[23] Unions that suffer from internal weakness (for example, incomplete organization) or external weakness (such as public pressure against stoppages in a public utility) are more willing to arbitrate. They reason that they can win a higher wage by arbitration than by the strike. One unidentified union leader, who is not generally attracted to wage arbitration, feels that his organization might make an exception depending upon "whether or not we were in position to strike."[24]

Several historical cases of union policies fortify this analysis. The United Mine Workers, which frequently engaged in wage arbitration at the turn of the century and during World War I, rejected such a bid by the operators as well as President Harding's urgent request during the 1922 wage dispute. "Union miners," their spokesmen declared, "still possess their one powerful weapon of defense—the strike. . . . If arbitration were accepted as a principle in the coal mining industry, the miner would lose his last means of defense."[25] In 1919, the Haverhill, Massachusetts shoe workers accepted arbitration after many years of opposition. Earlier, the union had been dominated by highly skilled turn workmen who were certain of their own power. The introduction of McKay machinery, by diluting skills, had reduced their strength and thereby laid the basis for a new policy. Similarly, the New York City printing trades, exhausted by prolonged strikes and lockouts over the forty-four hour week, embraced arbitration after 1906 in order to recover their strength.[26]

The tactical use of arbitration is evident in other aspects of union policy, such as "buck-passing" and the insincere offer to arbitrate. Organizations that want to avoid assuming political responsibility with their members for wage settlements they recognize as inevitable often pass the burden of decision to an arbitrator. Similarly, unions that intend to strike and seek public support for the stoppage sometimes offer to arbitrate under conditions they know are unacceptable to the employer. They might insist, for example, upon submitting both wages and union security, knowing that management regarded the latter as inarbitrable. The employer would then have to bear the onus with the public for having rejected arbitration.

[23] Quoted in Woytinsky, *op. cit.*, p. 60.
[24] Quoted in *ibid.*, p. 59.
[25] Quoted in Vertrees J. Wyckoff, *The Wage Policies of Labor Organizations in a Period of Industrial Depression* (Baltimore: Johns Hopkins Press, 1926), pp. 91, 94.
[26] Norton, *op. cit.*, pp. 201–202; Bogardus, *op. cit.*, pp. 39–40.

The management view of wage arbitration is similar, revealing the double edge of that instrument. Sophisticated employers who recognize the inadequacy of their bargaining power prefer arbitration to a strike or lockout. The New York Printers League, for example, urged this procedure upon the printing trades in 1907 because it was a new and experimental employers' association that controlled only a small segment of the industry. The League felt that arbitration would offer an opportunity to enhance its strength and prestige.[27] Management, furthermore, sometimes prefers that an outsider assume the responsibility for a wage change. An illustration is the executive who stated that he was quite willing to negotiate on a wage increase that was not unduly costly to the firm. "But if the amount was, say, $10,000,000, I think it would be better for the stockholders and for the public to have the arbitrator decide."[28] Employers in the regulated public utilities commonly insist upon the formality of wage arbitration to buttress their case for a rate or fare increase. Finally, in urban transit disputes retailers and the newspapers often press the employers to take arbitration rather than a strike.

The Webbs have fitted arbitration into the framework of collective bargaining in this fashion:

> There is no magic in the fiat of an arbitrator as a remedy for strikes and lockouts. If either party really prefers fighting . . . there will be no submission to arbitration. If both parties are willing to bargain, and are sufficiently well organized and well educated to be capable of it, no outside intervention will be needed.[29]

Hence wage arbitration can exist only within the structure of the bargaining system.

If arbitrators possessed a monopoly over definitive criteria of wage determination, they would undoubtedly decide many more cases. They are, however, no more omniscient in the handling of these standards than the parties and, more important, the criteria themselves are open to fundamental question.

Man's noble quest for certainty, for the general law to explain the variety of the universe, has led him into an endless search for the bases of wage phenomena. The appeal to reason has been grounded upon the yearning for a good society. If it were possible to generalize the elements of a fair wage, equity would prevail and disputes over wages would be unnecessary. At an earlier and more innocent time, Stockett could write:

---

[27] Bogardus, *op. cit.*, p. 40.
[28] Quoted in Woytinsky, *op. cit.*, p. 63.
[29] Sidney and Beatrice Webb, *Industrial Democracy* (2d ed.; London: Longmans, Green, 1920), pp. 239–240.

The arbitrator's function partakes of a judicial nature; the decision rendered must be based upon some definite, accepted principle of reason governing the disputed question. There is nothing, therefore, in the method of arbitration to prevent the attainment of a permanent solution of the wage problem—a solution, in that the underlying causes of the wage dispute are met by the application of a reasonable principle of wages; and permanent, in that this principle is always applicable. . . .[30]

The experience with wage determination leaves no doubt that this hopeful view expects too much of the real world. Arbitrators have repeatedly noted that there are no generally accepted standards for fixing wages, that the problem does not lend itself to expression in a mathematical formula. "It is no secret," Brown has observed, "that there exists no general agreement on the criteria that should or do determine the level of wages."[31] In the same vein, Soule has written that "society is substantially agreed that murder is a crime, but society is not substantially agreed as to what circumstances, and how much, wages should be raised."[32]

Further, the parties and arbitrators often cite criteria to rationalize a decision they already have made. A union, for example, may insist upon a ten-cent increase because a rival has won that amount, but may justify it on the grounds of cost of living. In addition, the standards, though inherently neutral, may be adapted to partisan purposes. As a consequence, unions and management are their fair-weather friends, citing them when it is advantageous to do so and repudiating them when that serves self-interest. Management, by way of illustration, may insist upon inability to pay in bad times and urge the irrelevancy of ability to pay in good times.

Finally, placing sole reliance upon any one criterion ultimately leads to absurdity. If wages, for example, were adjusted in accordance with productivity alone, technologically advancing industries would in time create inequitable differentials over stagnant industries. If cost of living were the sole factor, real wages could not advance in a progressive economy. The same conclusion applies to the other standards.

This analysis may suggest that the orthodox criteria are irrelevant to wage determination. Such a conclusion is unwarranted, since they lie close to the heart of wage-fixing. Their applicability is unquestioned; the manner in which they are applied is the challenging exercise in judgment. For they require decisions of policy rather than of fact; the former are invariably and the latter are seldom in dispute. The core problem for the wage arbitrator is to balance conflicting standards. The possible range of solutions that these factors afford is normally

[30] Stockett, *op. cit.*, p. xiii.
[31] Fall River Textile Mfrs. Assn. and Textile Workers, 11 *LA* 988 (1949).
[32] Soule, *op. cit.*, p. 4.

greater than the bargaining difference between the parties. Hence the arbitrator must allocate weight to them in order to produce an award within this difference. As Dunlop has written in the context of a typical case:

> The Union pointed to higher rates in some companies and localities; the Company referred to lower rates in other situations. The Union cited the rise in living costs from the first postwar negotiations; the Company pointed to the comparative movement of wage rates and living costs from earlier dates. The Union held that these employees are entitled to the "normal" increase in productivity in American industry; the Company insisted it cannot afford any further wage rate increase. As is normally the case in wage issues, the parties have appealed to conflicting standards or have applied a proposed criterion in conflicting ways.
>
> The problem presented to the Arbitration Board is consequently that of appraising and balancing conflicting standards. The task is how much weight to give to one standard as compared to another. The case presents no serious dispute over facts.... The decision must consequently be a judgment of the relative significance to be assigned to each of the standards proposed by the parties.[33]

With these preliminaries out of the way, the ground has been prepared for a full-scale analysis of wage arbitration. The chapter that follows is concerned with the institutional features of that process.

---

[33] Indianapolis Railways and Amalgamated Street Railway Employees, 9 *LA* 328 (1947). Faced with a conflict between the industry pattern and the employers' doubtful financial condition in another case, Healy observed: "In reconciling these two, the arbitrator confesses that his decision is the product of an attempt to balance two uncertain, but nevertheless real, considerations." Merchandise Warehouses of Boston and Longshoremen, 6 *LA* 525 (1946).

II. WAGE ARBITRATION: THE INSTITUTION[1]

1. *In General*

THE PRECEDING discussion suggests the conclusion that wage arbitration plays a secondary role, at best, in collective bargaining as practiced in the United States. Although this result cannot be substantiated precisely because of the limitations of available statistics, there is no room for reasonable doubt. The number of reported awards averaged about forty annually in the period 1945–1950, the peak year being 1946 with sixty-four. A spot check of six leading arbitrators in various parts of the country indicates that perhaps one in four awards is published. In the years 1945–1950, these men arbitrated a total of seventy-four general wage disputes, of which eighteen (24 per cent) were reported. If their experience is representative of all arbitrators, the national average for those years would have been in the neighborhood of 150 to 200 wage cases per year. These figures, of course, constitute no more than a tiny fraction of the estimate of 100,000 agreements in effect. There is small risk in concluding that no more than 2 per cent of general wage changes in collective bargaining are arrived at through arbitration in peacetime.

The same general conclusion emerges when the problem is examined from another viewpoint, namely, the attitudes of the parties. In a national survey of those experienced in arbitration only 31 per cent of management people favored voluntary arbitration of contract terms (some excluded wages) as contrasted with 91 per cent who approved of grievance arbitration. Similarly, 47 per cent of the union spokesmen voted for the former, while 93 per cent were in favor of the latter.

---

[1] A note on method: This chapter is almost wholly and other sections of the study are in part based upon an analysis of published arbitration awards appearing in the Bureau of National Affairs' *Labor Arbitration Reports*, vols. 1–14, covering the period 1945–1950, in other words, from V-J Day to the Korean War. BNA was selected because its arbitration reports are more comprehensive than alternatives. The sample covers all the 209 reported decisions in which at least one issue involved a general change in the wage level and a final and binding award was handed down. Of this number, eighty-five are concerned exclusively with wages and 124 deal with that as well as other matters. Grievance arbitrations and fact-finding reports (including emergency board and board of inquiry reports) on wages are excluded. The period covered reflects a variety of conditions both with respect to the economy as a whole and for particular industries: inflation, stability, deflation. There is no reason to believe that the sample is unrepresentative of all the wage arbitrations that took place during this half-decade. BNA's policy, according to its associate editor, is to publish all the general wage awards it can obtain, provided that the arbitrator gives his reasoning. It makes special efforts to acquire wage decisions. All the tables in this chapter derive from this source.

[14]

Furthermore, the comments of those who approved of contract arbitration made it clear that they wished it used sparingly.[2]

2. *Industry Distribution*

The industry distribution of wage arbitration is significant, both for those that use it and those that do not. The reported awards in the period 1945–1950, break down by industry as shown in table 1.

TABLE 1

INDUSTRY DISTRIBUTION OF REPORTED AWARDS, 1945–1950

	Number
Urban transit	37
Heat, light, power, and water	19
Wholesale and retail trade	19
Water transportation	17
Printing and publishing	11
Textile mill products	11
Communication	8
Electrical machinery, equipment, supplies	7
Construction	6
Apparel	6
Food and kindred products	6
Furniture and fixtures	6
Machinery (except electrical)	5
Services	5
Other (fewer than 5)	43
Unclassified	3
Total	209

The transit industry leads all others by a wide margin. It is followed by three bunched together—heat, light, power, and water; trade; and water transportation. Another group—printing and publishing; textiles; and communication—are the remaining industries with substantial representation.

A second method of looking at this distribution is by grouping industries into categories that practice wage arbitration. They are shown in table 2.

These figures clearly establish the fact that among the users of wage arbitration those industries which directly affect the public are much the most important. About three of every five cases in the sample oc-

---

[2] Edgar L. Warren and Irving Bernstein, "A Profile of Labor Arbitration," *Industrial and Labor Relations Review*, IV (January, 1951), 202–203. A more limited study of labor-management opinion by the Twentieth Century Fund substantiates the doubts the parties reserve for contract arbitration. W. S. Woytinsky and Associates, *Labor and Management Look at Collective Bargaining* (New York: Twentieth Century Fund, 1949), pp. 54–69.

curred in an industry in which a stoppage would have had an immediate impact upon consumers. Of these, the general public utility category is much more important than the nonutility group. When to these two is added the third, industries which have engaged in wage arbitration for many years, three of every four cases are accounted for.

TABLE 2
INDUSTRY GROUP DISTRIBUTION OF REPORTED AWARDS, 1945–1950

I. *Public utilities*	Number	Per cent
Urban transit	37	17.7
Heat, light, power, and water	19	9.1
Water transportation	17	8.1
Communication	8	3.8
Warehousing and storage	4	1.9
Air transportation	3	1.4
Railroads	3	1.4
Highway transportation	2	1.0
Medical and health services	1	0.5
Educational services	1	0.5
Subtotal	95	45.4
II. *Nonutility industries directly affecting public*		
Wholesale and retail trade	19	9.1
Services	5	2.4
Hotels	3	1.4
Subtotal	27	12.9
III. *Other industries in which arbitration historically practiced*		
Textile mill products	11	5.3
Printing and publishing	11	5.3
Construction	6	2.9
Apparel	6	2.9
Leather	3	1.4
Subtotal	37	17.8
Grand total	159	76.1

Since these three categories together comprise no more than a fraction of the American economy, it is apparent that many industries either do not practice wage arbitration at all or use it very rarely. This is true of the mining group—coal, metals, petroleum, and natural gas. More important, with certain light industry exceptions, the great manufacturing category does not use wage arbitration. This can be said of steel and other metal production and fabrication, of automobile, airframe, and other transportation equipment manufacture, of rubber, of chemicals, of paper, and of tobacco. The finance and insurance category reveals a similar disinclination to employ this procedure. It may be concluded from this analysis that the great majority of large enterprises (excepting some public utilities) do not arbitrate wage changes, in fact, do not arbitrate contract alterations of any sort.

This result finds substantiation in a breakdown of the seventy-seven cases for which employment data are available. Only nine involved five thousand or more employees. Of these, five were public utilities, two were nonutilities but concerns dealing directly with consumers, and two were in manufacturing (food and hosiery). The influence of the New Jersey public utility statute is apparent, since four of the nine cases took place under that act, two involving the telephone company and two a large transit system. Aside from these, only one large firm, Campbell Soup, appeared among the remaining five, the other four involving employer associations. It may be added that thirty-nine of the seventy-seven cases involved fewer than five hundred workers. Large steel, nonferrous metals, automobile, electrical, aircraft, rubber, and oil companies, as well as the bituminous coal associations, are conspicuously absent.

The high incidence of this procedure in the public utilities stems from a recognition by both management and unions in these industries that wage arbitration, regardless of inherent limitations, is preferable to a work stoppage. In most cases, both accept the idea that the public health and safety, or at least its convenience, cannot long be jeopardized. As a consequence, unions hesitate to call strikes for fear of losing public sympathy. Further, governmental authority—federal, state, and local— cannot and will not tolerate a stoppage beyond the point where general suffering begins, and usually acts before that condition prevails. Hence the "right" of a public utility union to strike is severely circumscribed as compared with organizations in less essential fields, and the union can often get "more" by arbitration. By the same token, utility management is less willing to permit a stoppage to take place and thereby incur public wrath. Consumers, particularly within the business community, urge the utilities to concede. Finally, and perhaps most important, an increase in rates based upon higher wage costs resulting from an award is more readily justified before a regulatory body than one flowing from a joint agreement. A utility executive, for example, has pointed out that an arbitration "relieves the management of responsibility for a rate increase."[3]

---

[3] Quoted in Woytinsky, *op. cit.*, p. 63. Several arbitrators have discussed the relationship of wage arbitration to the right to strike in utilities. See Capital Transit

3. *Union Distribution*

The unions that practice wage arbitration reflect both the forces generated within the industries of which they are a part and internal pressures. The distribution of unions in the sample is found in table 3. These statistics fortify the conclusion that union policy toward

TABLE 3
UNION DISTRIBUTION OF REPORTED AWARDS, 1945–1950

	Number
Street Railway Employees, AFL	29
Retail, Wholesale and Department Store Employees, CIO	11
Electrical, Radio and Machine Workers, CIO[1]	10
Electrical Workers, AFL	10
Teamsters, AFL	10
Transport Workers, CIO	8
Textile Workers, CIO	7
Utility Workers, CIO	6
Longshoremen and Warehousemen, CIO[1]	5
Furniture Workers, CIO	5
Machinists, AFL	4
Retail Clerks, AFL	4
Communications Assn., CIO[1]	4
Hotel and Restaurant Employees, AFL	4
Longshoremen, AFL[1]	3
Railway organizations, Ind. and AFL	3
Building trades, AFL	3
Textile Workers, AFL	3
Maritime Union, CIO	3
Office and Professional Workers, CIO[1]	3
Mine, Mill and Smelter Workers, CIO[1]	3
Printing Pressmen, AFL	3
Other (fewer than 3)	70
Total	211[2]

[1] Affiliation as of date of award.
[2] Exceeds 209 due to unions coöperating in two cases.

wage arbitration is inherently tactical. Powerful organizations that strike with impunity, such as the United Mine Workers, seldom, if ever, employ this procedure. The unions that do arbitrate are mainly of two types: those that contend with external pressure limiting the strike weapon and those that are internally weak. The former may or may not be organizationally weak; no one, by way of illustration, would accuse

Co. and Amalgamated Street Railway Employees, 9 *LA* 666 (1947); Puget Sound Navigation Co. and Masters, Mates and Pilots, 13 *LA* 255 (1949). In some utilities arbitration has become the prevailing method of fixing wages. At Puget Sound Navigation Co., for example, wages were arbitrated in 1940, 1947, 1948, and 1949.

the Street Railway Employees, the Teamsters, or the Longshoremen of suffering from that condition.

The incidence of unions in the first category, of course, appears most prominently in the utility field—the Street Railway Employees, the IBEW, some Teamster locals, the Transport Workers, the Utility Workers, and the Longshoremen. Nonutility unions in industries that deal directly with the public are also well represented—the Retail, Wholesale and Department Store Employees with eleven cases, the Hotel and Restaurant Employees with four, and the Retail Clerks with three.

Structural weakness also supplies an inducement to arbitrate. One study has concluded that it is favored "by some younger and weaker unions, perhaps because they believe their demands would be supported better by logic than by their bargaining power."[4] This is substantiated by the fact that seventeen (23 per cent) of the seventy-four unions that appear in the present group are either small independent internationals or locals unattached to internationals. Further evidence stems from the unusually high incidence of left-wing organizations. During this period, 1945–1950, eleven of the seventy-four unions were either Communist-controlled or contained a significant left-wing element and together they accounted for about a fourth of all the cases in the sample. Since the likelihood is slim that the Communist party espouses the arbitration principle, it is safe to conclude that weak unions subject to its control calculated that they could be more effective wagewise by employing that device. Finally, organizations rent by factionalism or debilitated by jurisdictional disputes can win time to recover by substituting arbitration for conflict with the employer. This is the case with the Los Angeles Retail Clerks union that engaged in several years of jurisdictional struggle with the Teamsters. In 1950, the former entered into a five-year contract with a large employers' association which requires the arbitration of wages if the parties fail to agree at the annual reopenings.[5]

4. *Time Cycles*

The statistical sample necessarily covers so short a span that it can be only suggestive with respect to the temporal patterns in the use of wage arbitration. Further, much of the period was marked by unusual postwar economic adjustments. The annual distribution of awards is revealed in table 4.

---

[4] Woytinsky, *op. cit.*, p. xvii.

[5] There is evidence that the Australian arbitration system has enhanced the bargaining power of weak unions. Wilson Compton, "Wage Theories in Industrial Arbitration," *American Economic Review*, VI (July, 1916), 334.

These figures suggest that the incidence of wage arbitration may be positively correlated with price movements. The years 1946–1947 constitute the peak in case load and represent a time of full employment and a rapidly rising price level. The postwar "recession" of 1948–1949, with an accompanying price decline, witnessed a sharp drop in the volume of arbitrations.[6]

TABLE 4
ANNUAL DISTRIBUTION OF REPORTED AWARDS, 1945–1950

	Number
1945 (part of year)	3
1946	64
1947	61
1948	40
1949	29
1950 (part of year)	12
Total	209

If this relationship to prices extends to the business cycle as well, an intriguing question remains unanswered: why is there not a higher incidence of wage arbitrations during depression? On its face, there would seem to be several reasons for a high volume of awards at the bottom of the cycle. In the first place, unions are reluctant to strike at such a time for fear of defeat and might welcome an alternative. Second, arbitration is a useful device for labor organizations to avoid political responsibility for the wage cuts that accompany depressions. Hence they might turn to it at such times for the purpose of "saving face."

[6] This cyclical pattern appeared as well in the World War I era, as reported in chapter i. Specificity is possible in the case of the New York book and job printing industry, for which wage arbitration data are available for the period 1911–1925:

1911	1
1912–1916	0
1917	1
1918	2
1919	0
1920	9
1921	10
1922	1
1923	1
1924	0
1925	4
Total	29

Here again, the peak years were in the postwar inflation and the case load dropped sharply in the following periods of deflation and price stability. James F. Bogardus, *Industrial Arbitration in the Book and Job Printing Industry of New York City* (Philadelphia: University of Pennsylvania Press, 1934), p. 98.

5. *Locality Distribution*

The distribution of wage arbitrations by locality, as shown in table 5, reveals a high concentration in a few areas.

New York, of course, is far in the lead with a fourth of all the reported cases. New Jersey and California also have heavy representa-

TABLE 5

LOCALITY DISTRIBUTION OF REPORTED AWARDS, 1945–1950

	Number
New York	55
New Jersey	29
California	23
Pennsylvania	13
Massachusetts	11
Nation-wide	9
Washington	7
District of Columbia	7
Ohio	5
Atlantic and Gulf Coast	5
Missouri	5
Other (fewer than 5)	38
Unknown	2
Total	209

TABLE 6

REGIONAL DISTRIBUTION OF REPORTED AWARDS, 1945–1950

	Number
Middle Atlantic	105
Pacific	34
Midwest	26
New England	18
South	9
Mountain	1
Interregional	14
Unknown	2
Total	209

tion. The regional patterns suggested become more apparent when the data are rearranged as in table 6.

The practice of wage arbitration is largely confined to the east and west coasts of the United States. The New England and Middle Atlantic states together account for 58.9 per cent and the Pacific Coast states for 16.3 per cent of the total, a combined percentage of 75.2. Both the Southern and Mountain areas reveal an expected low incidence, but the Midwest falls in this category as well.

The reasons for this distribution are varied and not entirely clear.

It would be an oversimplification, for example, to link a high incidence of wage arbitration to the maturity of collective bargaining, or, for that matter, to its youth. Both New York City, where bargaining is long established, and Los Angeles, where it is of recent origin, have a good many cases. Some of the factors that help to explain this geographical distribution are these:

The industrial character of an area tends to be reflected in the incidence of wage arbitration. In other words, communities like New York and Los Angeles are dominated by light industries with small or medium-sized units which, in turn, tend to rely on this process. Districts in which large firms in heavy industries prevail, for example, Pittsburgh and Detroit, do not use arbitration to fix wages. In the case of New York, the success of the State Board of Mediation as an appointing agency has undoubtedly been an added factor. In New Jersey the public utility statute has produced a good many cases.

6. *Appointing Agency Distribution*

The distribution of agencies that either appointed or assisted in the selection of arbitrators in wage cases is as shown in table 7.

TABLE 7

APPOINTING AGENCY DISTRIBUTION OF REPORTED AWARDS, 1945–1950

		Number
Parties		59
Federal Mediation & Conciliation Service (Conciliation Service, before 1947)		45
State mediation boards		
	New York ... 14	
	New Jersey ... 11	
	Connecticut ... 3	
	Wisconsin ... 2	
	Total	30
Secretary of Labor		14
American Arbitration Association		9
National Mediation Board		5
Governor		5
Court		3
National Wage Stabilization Board		2
Mayor		2
National War Labor Board		1
Mayor, U. S. District Court, State Supreme Court		1
Unknown		33
Total		209

The three most important agencies by far are the parties themselves, the Federal Mediation Service, and the state mediation boards. It is hardly surprising that unions and management should prefer to select their own arbitrators in a matter as significant as wages. Among the agencies that operate nationally, the Mediation Service is the leader by a wide margin. Apparently the American Arbitration Association designates relatively fewer arbitrators in general wage disputes than it does in grievance cases. Among the state agencies, New York and New Jersey are most active and, when Connecticut is added, form a heavy concentration about the New York City area. Important public officials at the

TABLE 8

STRUCTURAL FORM DISTRIBUTION OF REPORTED AWARDS, 1945–1950

All-neutral	*Number*	
1 neutral 126		
3 neutrals 7		
		133
Tripartite		
1 neutral, 1 labor, 1 employer 55		
1-2-2 9		
3-1-1 8		
2-2-2 2		
1-3-3 2		
		76
Total 209		

federal, state, and local levels together do not constitute a major source of appointments. The same may be said of judges, and both groups seem to be losing ground. It is worth noting that in four situations the parties named their grievance umpire to serve in a wage dispute.

7. *Structural Form Distribution*

An arbitration body may be one of two basic types: all-neutral or tripartite. With the former, only the neutral member (or members) has a vote. In a tripartite arrangement, on the other hand, the neutral, labor, and employer member (or members) cast a vote. There are a variety of combinations possible in composing an arbitration body and their distribution in the sample is shown in table 8.

The all-neutral structure is almost twice as popular as the tripartite system in the wage cases studied. Of the former, almost all are one-man arrangements. There has been considerable experimentation with tripartite board forms in wage disputes—equal representation for each group (1-1-1 and 2-2-2), superior representation for the neutrals (3-1-1), and superior representation for the partisans (1-2-2 and 1-3-3). Here again, the simplest form (1-1-1) is the favorite by a wide margin.

In an all-neutral system, particularly when it consists of a single man, there is no problem of authority to render a decision. With tripartitism, on the contrary, it is necessary to determine at the outset whether the board will operate under the majority rule or unanimity principle. Virtually all the cases in the sample necessitated a majority vote in order to reach a decision. This required that the neutral member (s) agree with one or both partisan(s)—with one structural exception—in order to issue an award. A dissatisfied partisan(s) was, of course, free to dissent. The distribution of tripartite board divisions is shown in table 9.

TABLE 9

TRIPARTITE BOARD DIVISIONS IN REPORTED AWARDS, 1945–1950

	Number
Unanimous	9
Employer dissent	34
Union dissent	29
Employer and union dissent[1]	4
Total	76

[1] In a 3-1-1 structure in which each member casts one vote the neutrals alone control a majority, leaving both partisans free to disagree.

Under tripartite systems it is rare for wage awards to be issued unanimously. The great majority include a dissent by one side or the other and occasionally by both. In this sample, employers tended to dissent a bit more frequently than unions. Their closeness to each other, however, is more impressive statistically than the difference between them.

8. *Money Distribution of Awards*

Many question whether arbitrators tend to favor unions or management in their decisions. In a large number of cases (particularly grievance matters) it is either difficult or impossible to obtain an answer because victory and defeat are not measurable. Wage decisions, at least, do not suffer this disadvantage because they are expressed in quantitative form. It should be emphasized, however, that even here the immeasurable and unknown factors that affect a given case can be important. Hence this effort to evaluate the money distribution of awards must be no more than a rough guide to the behavior of arbitrators.

In 103 cases in the sample the union's demand, the employer's offer, and the arbitrator's award were all expressed in cents per hour (rather than per cent). Where the history of negotiations was reported, last offers and demands were chosen. These data yielded the spread between the parties' positions and permitted a translation of the award into a percentage of this difference. For example, if a union had asked fifteen cents and the employer had offered five, the spread was ten cents; an award of ten cents would be 50 per cent of this difference.

In these 103 awards the arbitrator granted 100 per cent of the difference, that is, ruled wholly for the union, in eleven cases, and

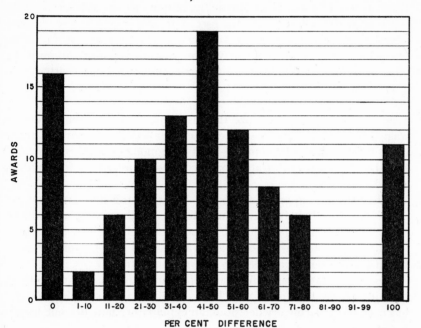

Fig. 1. Distribution of 103 awards as per cent of difference between parties.

granted zero per cent, that is, sided entirely with the employer, in sixteen decisions. This meant that the great majority, seventy-six, were split.

The distribution of these 103 awards is shown in figure 1. The money awards, expressed as a per cent of the difference between union and employer, are grouped in class intervals of 10 per cent (except for the terminals).

This distribution reveals a peak near the midpoint as well as a significant incidence of awards at both terminals. In other words, arbitrators most frequently grant an amount that is between 25 and 75 per cent of the spread between the parties. In addition, they quite often side entirely with one position or the other. They rarely, however, award amounts between the extremes and the central area. It is to be noted that there is a moderate weighting in favor of employers.

A similar result appears by averaging the awards. Arbitrators granted an average award of 43.7 per cent of the difference in all 103 cases. That is to say, they approximated the midpoint between the parties with a slight weighting in the direction of the management position. It seems that arbitrators are inclined to grant a somewhat larger amount when wages alone are submitted than when a variety of issues come before them. In the fifty-eight cases involving only wages the average was 45.3 per cent of the difference. In the forty-five cases in which several issues were before them the wage award averaged 41.5 per cent of the difference. This suggests that a slightly lower amount is granted in multiple issue decisions as compensation for concessions on other matters.

9. Incidence of Criteria

Wage-determining criteria are the instruments of decision-making in wage arbitration. They constitute the elements that union and management fashion into arguments to justify the money positions they take. Equally important, arbitrators balance these standards in formulating awards.

It is, therefore, appropriate to ask: What are the standards that are cited? What is their incidence in general? Are there significant differences between unions, employers, and arbitrators in their use? To which standards do the parties and arbitrators lend the greatest weight? Finally, does their incidence vary between industries?

The 209 reported cases afford an opportunity to seek answers to these questions. Since the analysis has been encumbered by complexities and has necessitated arbitrary decisions, an explanatory note of some length is required.

In 195 of the 209 reported awards, the arbitrator set forth, at least in part, the standards he and the parties advanced formally to justify their positions. Unions, employers, and arbitrators together cited criteria on 1,027 occasions in these 195 cases. These items represent only affirmative contentions, that is, rebuttal arguments are excluded. For example, a union's citation of the rising cost of living as a ground for wage advance is included, but the employer's view that it should be ignored is omitted. In addition, in 114 of the cases the arbitrator explicitly declared that one standard received sole or primary weight in the award.

Naturally, neutrals differ markedly in the completeness of their reporting. As a consequence, unstated and implicitly rejected factors were not reflected in the data. It is reasonable to assume, however, that even if the unknown considerations had been included the results would not differ significantly. This assumption is based upon the size of the sample and the fact that the conclusions square with what is known from other sources.

These 1,027 citations of criteria have been classified into ten categories defined as follows:

1. *Comparisons*—an increase or decrease is justified by comparison with wage levels or wage changes in other firms in the industry (intraindustry), other industries (interindustry), other plants of the same company (intracompany), other locals of the union (intraunion), or other unions (interunion).

2. *Cost of living*—a movement up or down in an index of consumer prices is the basis for a wage adjustment in the same direction.

3. *Financial condition of the employer*—the firm's ability to pay, inability to pay, or price and competitive position merits a given course of wage action.

4. *Differential features of the work*—special conditions of employment should be reflected in the wage decision. Such factors include skill and physical strain differentials, availability of overtime and fringe benefits, unusual consequences of the method of wage payment, and time equities.

5. *Substandards*—existing rates are below a standard of "health and decency" or an "American" standard of living and should be raised to approach or reach one of the established budget levels.

6. *Productivity*—output per man-hour has risen (or declined) within the firm, the industry, or industry generally and wages should reflect this change.

7. *Hours-of-work factor*—regularity of employment or the length of the work week should affect the general wage level.

8. *General economic considerations*—a given wage adjustment, up or down, would have a favorable or unfavorable effect upon the economy as a whole. For example, it would be inflationary in a period of rising prices or it would place purchasing power in the hands of consumers at a time of deflation.

9. *Union behavior*—the union's strike record, good or bad, should be rewarded or penalized in the wage decision.

10. *Manpower attraction*—the existing rates are sufficiently high to recruit a labor supply; hence no increase is warranted.

It is to be emphasized that these criteria are classified in the terms in which the parties and the arbitrators themselves expressed them; it was not possible to look behind their statements. This policy has obviated both direct and indirect complications. An example of the former is an intraunion comparison which is simultaneously an intracompany comparison. In this case it would be classified in the category in which it was framed. An illustration of the indirect type of difficulty is an interindustry comparison which stems from a cost-of-living increase in the activating industry. Here also, it would be considered in the form in which the stating party had expressed it.

All the citations included are substantive, that is, they constitute

TABLE 10—INCIDENCE OF CRIT

Group	Comparisons			
	Intraindustry		Interindustry	
	Number	Per cent	Number	Per ce
Union.................................	98	26.2	71	19.
Employer..............................	81	28.9	28	10.
Arbitrator.............................	128	34.3	43	11.
Total.............................	307	29.9	142	13.
Arbitrator: first rankings..................	56	49.1	9	7.

Group	Cost of living		Financial condition of the employer [1]		Differential features of the work [2]		Substandard	
	Number	Per cent	Number	Per cent	Number	Per cent	Number	Per c
Union..........	97	25.9	11	2.9	11	2.9	32	8
Employer.......	21	7.5	89	31.8	32	11.4	1	0
Arbitrator.......	106	28.4	44	11.8	14	3.8	5	1
Total.........	224	21.8	144	14.0	57	5.6	38	3
Arbitrator: first rankings.......	39	34.2	4	3.5	1	0.9	2	1

[1] Ability to pay, inability to pay, effect of a wage change on the firm's prices and competitive position.
[2] Includes skill and physical strain differentials, availability of overtime and fringe benefits, special results c method of wage payment, and time equities.

affirmative arguments to justify a particular wage policy—up, down, or no change. Technical questions of application and procedural considerations are excluded. Contentions, for example, that a specific base date for measuring consumer price changes should be employed or that the language of the contract reopening clause is a bar to a standard are omitted from consideration.

The net effect here of these methodological decisions is to concentrate upon the broad substantive criteria of wage determination. Fuller treatment of secondary matters is reserved for later chapters.

A final word may be added concerning the impact of these procedures upon the relative validity of the sample breakdowns. Quite clearly, arbitrators' explicit first rankings are of greatest value as a guide to behavior. Among the three groups, as a whole, it is likely that the arbitrator category is more meaningful than the union and the union

ED IN WAGE ARBITRATION, 1945-1950

Comparisons							
Intracompany		Intraunion		Interunion		Total	
Number	Per cent	Number	Per cent	Number	Per cent	Number	Per cent
6	1.6	8	2.1	3	0.8	186	49.7
4	1.4	4	1.4	6	2.1	123	43.9
10	2.7	3	0.8	6	1.6	190	50.9
20	1.9	15	1.5	15	1.5	499	48.6
0	0	0	0	3	2.6	68	59.6

Productivity		Hours-of-work factor		General economic considerations[3]		Union behavior[4]		Manpower attraction[5]		Total	
Number	Per cent	Number	Per cent	Number	Per cent	Number	Per cent	Number	Per cent	Number	Per cent
16	4.3	11	2.9	8	2.1	2	0.5	0	0	374	99.8
4	1.4	0	0	6	2.1	1	0.4	3	1.1	280	99.9
5	1.3	9	2.4	0	0	0	0	0	0	373	99.9
25	2.4	20	1.9	14	1.4	3	0.3	3	0.3	1,027	100
0	0	0	0	0	0	0	0	0	0	114	100

[3] The general economic consequences of a wage adjustment, for example, that it will be inflationary or will create consumer purchasing power.
[4] The union's strike record, good or bad, should affect the wage decision.
[5] Existing wage rates are high enough to recruit a labor force.

more so than the employer. Arbitrators, in other words, are assumed to cite criteria to which they genuinely lend weight more regularly than either of the others, and employers emphasize excluded negative standards more often than unions.

With methodological preliminaries out of the way, we may now turn to the results. The incidence of these 1,027 citations of criteria in the 195 awards for which information is available is shown in table 10. The results expressed in percentage terms are presented graphically in figures 2 and 3.

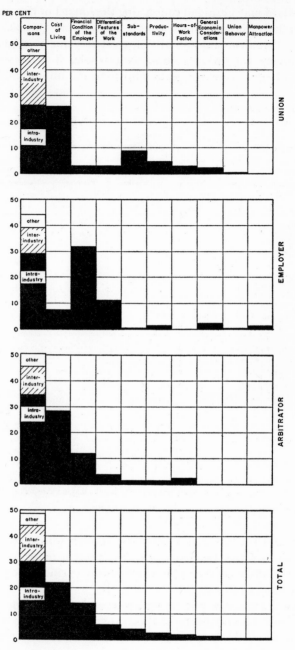

Fig. 2. Incidence of criteria cited in wage arbitration, 1945–1950.

Considered from the standpoint of the distribution of citations among the ten criteria, the totals for all three groups reveal a significant concentration. Approximately half the 1,027 items consisted of comparisons. Of these comparisons, intraindustry ones were by far the most important, while interindustry ones were used fairly often. Intracompany, intraunion, and interunion comparisons were rarely cited. The second standard, cost of living, accounted for just over one-fifth of the

PER CENT

	Compar-isons	Cost of Living	Financial Condition of the Employer	Differential Features of the Work	Sub-standards	Produc-tivity	Hours-of-Work Factor	General Economic Consider-ations	Union Behavior	Manpower Attraction
60										
50	other / inter-industry									
40										
30	intra-industry									
20										
10										
0										

Fig. 3. Incidence of criteria ranked first by arbitrators, 1945–1950.

total. Financial condition of the employer represented about one-seventh, followed by differential features of the work with about one-seventeenth. The remaining six criteria each constituted no more than an insignificant fraction of the total. Together, comparisons, cost of living, and financial condition comprised 85 per cent of all citations. At bottom, therefore, wage arbitration as represented by these cases revolved about these three fundamental considerations.

The distribution between the three groups suggests areas both of agreement and of disagreement. All groups relied very heavily upon comparisons. The intraindustry variety was far in the lead. Arbitrators placed greatest reliance upon this type, followed in order by employers and unions. Labor organizations revealed a substantially greater enthusiasm for interindustry comparisons than did either of the others. The remaining categories of comparisons were little cited by any group.

Arbitrators lent greater weight to the cost-of-living factor than did the other groups. They were followed closely by unions. Employers, in contrast, cited this argument less frequently. This difference is to be explained, in part at least, by the underlying economic conditions of 1945–1950. Although consumer prices declined moderately for part of the period, upward movement was the dominant characteristic. Hence the argument had greater general appeal to those seeking wage increases (unions).

Financial condition of the employer comprised almost a third of all employer citations. By contrast, arbitrators gave it weight in only about one-eighth of their contentions, while unions urged it hardly at all. Again, employers were far more prone than the others to emphasize differential features of the work, such as favorable fringe benefits. Substandards proved to be almost exclusively a union concern, employers giving it almost no emphasis and arbitrators very little. Much the same may be said of productivity. The hours-of-work factor, though rarely cited, was the concern only of unions and arbitrators. The remaining three won no favor from arbitrators and only a nod from the partisans.

Arbitrator first rankings, the most significant category, reveal an even greater shrinkage in the number of criteria emphasized. In 60 per cent of the 114 cases for which data are available, arbitrators based their decisions solely or primarily upon comparisons. Almost all of these were of the intraindustry type, with interindustry receiving modest and interunion a very small consideration. Neither intracompany nor intraunion comparisons won any favor. Approximately a third of these awards were based upon the cost of living. Finally, financial condition of the employer was the only other criterion to gain more than insignificant consideration and in that case only 3.5 per cent of the total. The conclusion—and it is striking—is that in those cases in which the arbitrator was influenced by a single standard, he relied almost wholly upon a comparison (normally intraindustry) or the cost of living. The other eight factors combined appeared in only seven of the 114 awards. This suggests that much of the argument in wage arbitration (and perhaps negotiations, as well) is window dressing.[7]

Refinement of the data by industry to determine deviations from the combined figures is hobbled by the smallness of the sample. The six industries represented by eleven or more awards were analyzed. In general, they followed the distribution for all industries. There were, however, a few differences that merit note.

---

[7] A Twentieth Century Fund survey of union and management views on the factors considered in negotiations in 1947–1948, as contrasted with this study's concern with actual argument in arbitration, produced generally similar conclusions. Woytinsky, *op. cit.*, pp. 73, 84.

In urban transit, arbitrators' first rankings lend considerably greater weight to intraindustry comparisons and hence to comparisons as a whole than in other industries, 78 as contrasted with 60 per cent. This is compensated for by a decline in the importance of the cost-of-living factor. The deviation, apparently, reflects the traditional practice in transit of basing adjustments primarily upon rates paid by other comparable systems, comparability determined by size of city.

A similar divergence crops up in printing and publishing, in which comparisons are of greater significance to all three groups. This is owing to a marked rise in the incidence of intra- and interunion as well as of intracompany comparisons. Presumably, this is to be explained largely by firmly established craft unionism with a consequent emphasis on comparability between locals and internationals in the printing trades. In water transportation, in contrast, arbitrators tend to rely more heavily upon cost of living than in industry generally. In textiles, the financial condition of the firm gained greater favor among arbitrators and employers than in the sample as a whole. This stems from the depressed condition of the industry during much of the period.

Having sketched the institutional characteristics of wage arbitration as practiced in this country, we now turn to a consideration of some of the procedural problems that accompany its employment.

III. SOME PROCEDURAL PROBLEMS

THE ARBITRATION of general wage changes, procedurally viewed, is very much like the arbitration of anything else. There is no need to duplicate a large existing literature. Hence the concern is exclusively with those areas in which wages create a procedural divergence that justifies particular consideration. The present chapter, as a consequence, is a series of brief essays on those problems that complicate the employment of arbitration in wage disputes.

1. *Bargaining Structure*

Wage arbitration accepts the structural forms evolved in collective bargaining. It may involve, therefore, any possible combination of structures—single firm and single union, single firm and multiunion, multiemployer and single union, multiemployer and multiunion. There are, in other words, no special structural problems inherent in the arbitration of wages.

Speaking generally, the more homogeneous the bargaining unit is for both parties, the greater the prospect of reaching a decision without complication. Or, to turn the coin over, diversity of interest on either or both sides of the table compounds the difficulties of the parties and of the arbitrator. In multiemployer bargaining, it has been pointed out, "Any common program which is evolved normally represents a compromise which, in varying degree, is distasteful to some portion of the participating employers. . . ."[1] Each firm's wage position is a function of its own operating conditions. Hence the multiemployer unit normally contains companies with varying wage policies stemming from such factors as different products, methods of production, systems of wage payment, and ratios of labor to total costs. Much the same may be said of multiunion bargaining structures.

Whether multiunit forms tend to arbitrate wage changes more or less readily than simpler structures is not known. One may argue a priori in opposite directions. The inherently greater difficulty in reaching any decision suggests that multiple units would be less willing to arbitrate. On the other hand, political considerations, particularly on the employer side, are more prevalent in multiple arrangements. Hence arbitration may serve the same institutional ends for employer associations that it often does for unions.

There is no doubt that multiunit wage arbitrations are common.

---

[1] Sylvester Garrett and L. Reed Tripp, *Management Problems Implicit in Multi-Employer Bargaining*, Industry-Wide Collective Bargaining Series (Philadelphia: University of Pennsylvania Press, 1949), p. 21.

Among the 209 reported cases in the period 1945–1950, there were seventy (33.5 per cent) multiemployer arbitrations of which nine (4.3 per cent) were also multiunion.

An interesting problem is whether the employer or union would be more likely to achieve a more favorable wage result by arbitrating separately rather than jointly. In other words, can a firm win a lower wage by going it alone and can a union gain a higher wage by a similar separatism? There is every likelihood that the result would be much the same in either case. The powerful force of the comparison would, doubtless, prevail. The standards that determined the decision for the majority of related firms (or unions) would probably be extended to the outlander. The reports contain numerous illustrations.[2] As Garrett and Tripp observe:

> Employers cannot avoid pressure toward uniformity merely by refraining from joint action. They may find, in fact, that their collective bargaining on an individual basis is largely a matter of conforming, as a minimum, to the results of another settlement between the same union and a leading employer in the industry.[3]

The decision to associate, therefore, should be based upon considerations other than fictitious wage advantage that might be assumed to accompany arbitration (or, for that matter, negotiations).

The bargaining structure, however, may affect the wage standards that can be applied to a particular dispute. In a case of true industry-wide bargaining, for example, the most important criterion of wage determination, the intraindustry comparison, becomes irrelevant. Emergency boards and arbitration bodies in the railroad industry have been denied the use of intrasystem comparisons for many years because all the rates in the industry were before them at once.[4]

2. *The Reopening Clause*

A problem which has provoked controversy is the scope of the arbitrator's authority when wages are before him under a reopening clause of a labor contract. That is, is he more restricted in an interim wage review than he would be if the agreement as a whole had expired?

The purpose of a reopening clause is typically to protect employees against significant changes in wage-determining criteria during the

---

[2] In a case involving one of the building trades the contractors argued that poor business justified a wage cut. The arbitrator rejected the contention on the ground that a decrease would unfairly discriminate against this craft. He then awarded the same increase won by several other trades. Mason Contractors' Assn. of Detroit and Bricklayers, 12 *LA* 909 (1949).

[3] Garrett and Tripp, *op. cit.*, p. 14.

[4] Frederic Meyers, "Criteria in the Making of Wage Decisions by 'Neutrals': The Railroads as a Case Study," *Industrial and Labor Relations Review*, IV (April, 1951), 346.

term of a contract. It serves this end without the necessity for renegotiation of the entire agreement. A typical provision in a one-year contract reads as follows:

The wage clause of this agreement can be reopened at the expiration of any 6-month period, without the reopening of this working agreement, upon written notice given by either party 30 days prior to the expiration of any 6-month period from the date of this agreement or any anniversary date of this agreement.[5]

A permissive reopening, like this one, does not assure agreement. Since the union's power to enforce its wage position depends upon the right to withdraw labor, such a clause is of little value in the face of a continuing no-strike pledge in another section of the contract. To overcome this difficulty, wage reopeners are often accompanied by either a waiver of the prohibition on stoppages or by a requirement to arbitrate if the parties cannot agree.

In light of the objective of these clauses, it is to be expected that their incidence would be a function of rapid economic change. They were, for example, little used before World War II, but came into vogue in the inflation following V-J Day. In fact, many of the wage arbitrations in the period 1945–1950 occurred under reopening clauses.

Some provisions, like that cited above, merely permit wages to be reconsidered at a given moment. Others, however, specify the conditions that precipitate reopening. Among the more prominent are changes in the cost of living, in government wage and price policy, in general economic conditions, in the company's competitive position, and in industry or area wage levels.[6] This specificity serves to narrow the arbitrator's authority.

Two schools have developed on the scope of arbitration under an interim reopening. One argues that, in the absence of an express bar in the contract or submission, the arbitrator may consider any standard he would have weighed in a new contract dispute. The other responds that an interim review is inherently restrictive, that the arbitrator may concern himself only with factors that have changed since the agreement was signed. In the published cases, this dispute has found the unions ranged on one side urging the broader position, facing employers joined with arbitrators on the other favoring a narrower viewpoint.

The latter position is sometimes referred to as the "erosion theory." This means, presumably, that the employees should be recompensed for that segment of income which has deteriorated since the contract took effect and no more. One of the parents of this concept has stated

---

[5] *Collective Bargaining Provisions, Wage Adjustment Plans,* Bureau of Labor Statistics, Bull. no. 908–909 (Washington: 1948), p. 21.

[6] *Ibid.,* pp. 22–29.

that the reopening clause is "a safety valve . . . to be used only to relieve either side from forces which have come into play since the parties elected to set the wage rates by their agreement."[7]

This conclusion rests upon a theory of the bargained contract, framed by Miller as follows:

> The wage standard . . . adopted [in the initial agreement] is the result of free collective bargaining by experienced and alert representatives of strong organizations. The assumption that the resulting rate properly reflects the wage determining factors which had evidenced themselves by that time is a valid one. . . . The assumption rests solidly upon the realistic fact that a collectively bargained wage rate, among other things, reflects the considered judgment of the parties as to the balance of their relative economic strengths at the time the contract was made. And a wage rate thus fixed by the parties themselves upon the basis of their in'imate knowledge of the merits of the claims of each, and the push and pull, compromise and trading which are the characteristic elements of the collective bargaining process, is properly considered the best evidence of the wage standard from which to evaluate in an interim wage review any subsequent changes in pertinent wage-determining factors.[8]

The union rebuttal rests upon the view that this is an unrealistic interpretation of bargaining. As one labor dissent argues:

> It is said that the parties in agreeing to the June 1, 1948, wage scale considered "all the factors then deemed available." There is not a shred of evidence in the record to support that statement. . . .
>
> The record is clear on how rough-hewn the last . . . increase . . . was. . . . That was just plain horse trading and counter-thumping. The majority knows full well that these "expert and highly intelligent union bargainers" and their counterparts among the Publishers, as the majority flatters them all, never made any pretense of negotiating the niceties of a rationally ordered and internally balanced wage structure and of modulated and synchronized wage movements. The anvil of bargaining is used for hammering, not choruses.[9]

The deep purple of this prose scarcely adulterates the logic of the erosion theory. Wage behavior, as has been noted before, is not invariably distinguished for rationality. Hence it would be asking for the

---

[7] David L. Cole, "Fixed Criteria in Wage Rate Arbitration," *Arbitration Journal*, III (Fall, 1948), 170.

[8] Waterfront Employers Assn. and Longshoremen and Warehousemen, 9 *LA* 175–176 (1947). Arbitrators, virtually without exception, have accepted this view of the reopening clause. See Waterfront Employers Assn. and Longshoremen and Warehousemen, 5 *LA* 758 (1946); Atlantic & Gulf Coast Shippers and Maritime Union, 9 *LA* 632 (1948); R. H. Macy & Co. and Retail, Wholesale and Department Store Union, 11 *LA* 450 (1948); Fall River Textile Mfrs. Assn. and Textile Workers, 11 *LA* 984 (1949); Marcalus Mfg. Co. and Pulp, Sulphite and Paper Mi'l Workers, 11 *LA* 1115 (1948); Newspaper Publishers Assn. and Printing Pressmen, 12 *LA* 448 (1949); Committee for Tanker Cos. and Marine Engineers, 12 *LA* 855 (1949); *New York World-Telegram* and Newspaper Guild, 12 *LA* 946 (1949); Publishers Assn. and Typographical Union, 12 *LA* 1136 (1949); Publishers Assn. and Brotherhood of Electrical Workers, 13 *LA* 700 (1949); Washington Woodcraft Corp. and Furniture Workers, 14 *LA* 242 (1950).

[9] Publishers Assn. and Typographical Union, 12 *LA* 1143, 1145 (1949).

moon to expect a decision to express a pretty balance of wage-determining criteria. What it does signify, rather, is an equilibrium of forces on the contract as a whole. The union conceded on wages in return for a point gained elsewhere. For paying the price of a long contract, it doubtless exacted a *quid pro quo*. By granting the union a wage advantage in midterm, the arbitrator erases a consideration that led the employer to accept the contract as a unit.

As cautious men, however, the very arbitrators who have formulated this notion of the interim review have stepped back from it. Cole has written: "One further question is always present and entitled to some consideration, even though it is not consistent with the wage reopening 'erosion' theory; is there some gross inequity which demands correction?"[10] One suspects that an elephant might squeeze through this hole.

The debate over the scope of authority resolves itself primarily into a consideration of criteria. The position of arbitrators serves to restrict the grounds for wage change. Further, the time lapse between the signing of the contract and its reopening on wages is short (normally less than a year) with consequent narrowing of the room for maneuver. As a result, most of the standards become irrelevant and the remainder are limited in application.

Under the "erosion" theory such general arguments as substandards of living and productivity cannot be given weight. They are disqualified either because they are presumed to have been disposed of during the negotiations or because their wage consequences are immeasurable in so short a time span. Similarly, the usefulness of comparisons is seriously impaired under reopening clauses. It is improper, arbitrators argue, to contrast the *level* of rates between firms, industries, or unions. The only value of this standard is in connection with *changes* in wages following the effective date of the agreement. By far the most important criterion, of course, is cost of living. In fact, a basic function of reopening is to shield employees against a prospective rise in retail prices. Even here there is narrowing, since the base date for computation must be that of the contract.[11]

The discussion thus far has assumed arbitration under a reopening clause without other restrictions. When, however, the parties draft a special submission agreement, it takes precedence over the scope rule. In the *Boker* case, for example, the submission required the arbitrator

---

[10] *New York World-Telegram* and Newspaper Guild, 12 *LA* 947 (1949). See also Newspaper Publishers Assn. and Printing Pressmen, 12 *LA* 448 (1949) and North American Aviation and Automobile Workers, 19 *LA* 76 (1952).

[11] Awards that illustrate this analysis of criteria are Waterfront Employers Assn. and Longshoremen and Warehousemen, 5 *LA* 758 (1946) and Atlantic & Gulf Coast Shippers and Maritime Union, 9 *LA* 632 (1948).

to apply five criteria, one of which entailed comparing wages with those in the industry for several years preceding the signing of the contract. In the hearing the company contended that the limitations of the reopening clause of the collective agreement precluded such a comparison. The arbitrator, of course, overruled this argument.[12]

3. The Submission Agreement

The reason for the relative rarity of wage arbitration rests on the parties' fear of entrusting so vital a matter to an outsider. Men flee from uncertainty, and the arbitration process is beclouded with imponderables. In some cases an extreme award could destroy a union or a firm. The instrument for discounting risk, for hedging against the unknown, is the submission agreement.

This device (often called the stipulation) has two essential elements: to empower the particular arbitrator to render a decision and to fix the borders of his authority. The first is of no interest here; his power in relation to the risks of the parties is the issue under consideration.

All the experts agree that the submission is a desirable precondition for arbitration. Beyond minimizing the possibility of an unacceptable award, it serves several added functions. "Disputes have an uncanny habit of changing in midstream and sometimes multiply, like the amoeba, during the hearing."[13] The submission particularizes the point at issue by clearing out the underbrush of extraneous substantive controversy. Further, the very process of framing the issue compels the parties to bargain intensively, something they may not have theretofore done. These negotiations tend to define more precisely the area of difference and to sharpen their arguments. Finally, the submission often makes for a speedy and orderly hearing.[14]

Disagreement, however, has arisen over prehearing concurrence on the wage criteria the arbitrator should apply. Taylor has urged this function for "the forgotten document of industrial relations," as he refers to the submission. "If the parties don't want to take the risk of an arbitrator's unguided judgment, . . . they should work out instructions or criteria that both believe should be followed by an arbitrator in deciding the particular case at issue."[15] No one, certainly, would regard this suggestion as anything but laudable. There are, however, serious

[12] H. Boker & Co. and Mine Workers, District 50, 12 *LA* 608 (1949).
[13] Jules J. Justin, "Arbitration: Proving Your Case," *Personnel*, XXIV (1948), 7.
[14] Benjamin Aaron, "The Relation between Fact-Finding and Arbitration" (unpublished MS, n.d.), chap. ii, p. 9.
[15] George W. Taylor, "Can Wages Be Left to Collective Bargaining?" *Wages, Prices and the National Welfare* (Berkeley and Los Angeles: Institute of Industrial Relations, 1948), p. 40.

practical difficulties in its application, some of which Taylor himself
recognizes. The employer's dissent in the *Capital Transit* case (Taylor
was the chairman) pointed out:

I think it quite improbable that such criteria could be agreed upon in advance.
If perchance such criteria were adopted by the parties it is unlikely that arbitration
would ensue because the field of differences would be so narrowed that an agreement would be almost inevitable. Thus, the appointment of an Arbitration Board
presupposes inability to agree on accepted criteria.[16]

In addition, there is real danger that the presentation of standards in
the submission will be so warped as to prevent an acceptable award. It
is possible, for example, for able counsel on one side to slip in a restric-
tion that denies the other its most telling argument. Or a submission
drawn in joint good faith may inadvertently bar consideration of a
key factor.[17] Finally, even the most carefully drawn submission on
criteria may fail to narrow the crucial difference, namely, the spread
between the parties in cents per hour.

This criticism is reinforced by an examination of the statutory experience with wage arbitration after World War I. That is, a law that
lays down principles of wage determination for arbitral bodies per-
forms the same function as a submission that establishes criteria for
arbitrators. The Transportation Act of 1920, for example, enjoined the
Railroad Labor Board to fix rates that were "just and reasonable." In
so doing, the agency was required to take into consideration seven of
the conventional standards. These "seven sisters" proved virtually useless to the Board in the wage disputes it faced. The related experience
of the Kansas Industrial Court was, if anything, worse. The statute
under which it operated was patterned after the Transportation Act
but had eight rather than seven criteria. The Court, however, never
made systematic use of them.[18]

This analysis suggests that attention should be diverted from standards to money. In a wage case, the fundamental fear on each side is
that the arbitrator will award more or fewer cents per hour than either
regards as acceptable. Enough has been said of the opportunistic attitudes of unions and employers toward criteria of wage determination

---

[16] Capital Transit Co. and Amalgamated Street Railway Employees, 9 *LA* 692
(1947).
[17] Soule reports that in the printing cases after World War I submissions so em-
barrassed arbitrators that they had to devise means of evading them. George Soule,
Wage Arbitration, Selected Cases, 1920–1924 (New York: Macmillan, 1928), p. 12.
[18] Domenico Gagliardo, *The Kansas Industrial Court* (Lawrence: University of
Kansas Press, 1941), p. 235; C. O. Fisher, *Use of Federal Power in Settlement of Railway Labor Disputes,* Bureau of Labor Statistics, Bull. no. 303 (Washington: 1922), p.
115; H. D. Wolf, *The Railroad Labor Board* (Chicago: University of Chicago Press,
1927), p. 124.

to demonstrate that they have little interest in elevating them to matters of principle. Hence the real area for reducing risk through the submission lies in fixing a range beyond which the arbitrator may not go. There would, of course, be tactical difficulties in narrowing the spread. In some situations the parties would refuse to move from their original positions, reasoning that any concession would become the point of departure for an arbitral compromise. The uncertainties of arbitration, however, constitute a lever to nudge them into the zone of real money difference.

It is vital that the cents-per-hour spread be narrowed as far as possible to achieve the purpose of the submission. If, for example, the union's first demand is twenty-five cents and the employer's first offer zero, there is nothing gained by directing the arbitrator to award within this quarter range. If, on the other hand, the union comes down to fifteen cents and the employer up to ten cents in negotiations, it certainly minimizes risk to require him to stay within this nickel spread.[19]

The money difference, where obtainable, is the key element that the submission to wage arbitration should contain. There are, in addition, several items, mainly oriented to form rather than to substance, that support the narrowing function of this instrument. When they are matters of agreement, the parties should instruct the arbitrator on whether they want the award expressed in cents or per cent, on whether they wish to avoid fractional cents in the resulting rates, on the coverage of the award with respect to the bargaining unit, on the effective date, and on the method of applying the increase to the wage payment system if there are complexities. Finally, under a general reopening clause which permits reconsideration of "wages," they should define that term in the submission. Does it exclude premiums, vacations, holidays, and so forth?[20]

4. *Tripartite Board vs. Single Arbitrator*

During the depression in 1921, the Chicago Building Construction Employers' Association and the Building Trades Council disagreed over the former's demand for a wage cut and the dispute went to arbi-

---

[19] The Handsakers suggest that it may be very difficult to get the parties to submit the difference between their best offers. At least one is likely to insist upon its "outside" expectations. Morrison and Marjorie Handsaker, *The Submission Agreement in Contract Arbitration,* Labor Relations Series (Philadelphia: University of Pennsylvania Press, 1952), p. 58.

[20] This writer served as arbitrator in a case in which the employer sought to reduce his labor force. The agreement prohibited the submission of "wages" to arbitration. The union argued that the manning provision of the contract, admittedly a cost factor, was part of "wages," hence beyond the arbitrator's jurisdiction. A half-day of hearing and an interim ruling (with dissenting opinion!) were needed to dispose of this irrelevance.

tration. The contractors urged a tripartite board, but the unions successfully insisted upon a single arbitrator. They chose Judge K. M.
Landis, who was then about to leave the federal bench to become
"czar" of baseball in the backwash of the Black Sox scandal. Landis,
to understate the matter, liberally interpreted his authority over wages.
He comprehensively revamped working rules in order to extirpate what
he considered monopolistic practices. Over the opposition of both
parties, he created wage differentials between crafts in which equality
had theretofore existed. He chopped twenty-two rates under the employers' demands, in many cases to substantially lower levels. Finally,
he fixed wages for unions not party to the arbitration including several
whose contracts had not expired.

The award produced chaos in the Chicago construction industry for
half a decade. The unions bitterly resisted its enforcement and many
contractors contrived means to evade compliance. "American Plan"
elements in the city used it as a lever to undermine a citadel of unionism. The bargaining structure in the industry was disrupted. Violence
broke out in the bombing of buildings and the killing of policemen.
"On both sides there was a longing for the system of collective dealing
of the pre-Landis days."[21]

The Landis award is a dramatic testimonial to the tripartite system.
Its advantages over a single arbitrator in a wage case are clear. At bottom, they come down to acceptability, information-sharing, and mediation, and the three are interwoven.

An essential of arbitration, as pointed out in chapter i, is compliance with the award, and structure is a means to this end. For certain matters, notably most grievances, many experts believe that a
single neutral is better adapted. In contract disputes, generally speaking, and especially in wage cases, the tripartite form is preferable. In
the typical system the neutral must win a majority to make a decision.
It is, therefore, impossible to render an award repugnant to both sides.
Further, participation by a representative of the minority in decision-
making tempers potential majority extremism. The neutral, in other
words, learns the objections of the loser before issuance of the award.
Hence the borderline of noncompliance is defined, which may not be
the case where he rules alone. Under the pressures of acceptability,
tripartitism drives the decision toward center, thereby reducing the
hazards of further Landis awards.

The advantage stemming from information-sharing works two ways:
the neutral learns what the parties really want (and don't want) and

[21] Royal E. Montgomery, *Industrial Relations in the Chicago Building Trades*
(Chicago: University of Chicago Press, 1927), pp. 237–307.

they know what he intends to do. Obviously, it is of importance that the arbitrator discover how much in cents per hour each side will "take." In fact, nothing else is as significant. It is entirely possible, however, to endure a dozen days of formal hearing without acquiring this knowledge. Lesser has plaintively noted, "The arbitrator wishes to emphasize ... that this award has been reached with practically no help from either party."[22] Partisan board members make it a virtual certainty that the neutral will be told how far they are prepared to go.[23] Further, the tripartite form is a means of making the often green arbitrator more sophisticated about the industry and the bargaining relationship.

The converse is that men shy from surprise. They yearn to know what is about to happen, and their eagerness is a direct function of its importance. In a matter as crucial as a general wage change the parties are more likely to live with an unpleasant award if it is broken to them in advance. A tripartite board disposes of the element of surprise by inviting the union and employer to share in the decision-making process.

If universal criteria of wage determination existed, there would be no need for compromise in wage arbitration. The void created by their absence is filled by the standard of acceptability. It, in turn, suggests mediation. In other words, the way to dispose of wage issues is by reference to what the parties must have rather than to abstractions. To gain a majority, "the neutral arbitrator's judgment tends to be influenced by tactical considerations necessary to bring the case to a conclusion."[24] An example is the Pittsburgh transit case. The chairman urged the amount of the Chicago adjustment, since it was made at the most comparable property. Neither partisan board member, however, would go along. To obtain a majority, therefore, he was compelled to side with the one who most closely approximated the Chicago settlement. "The Chairman presents no logical defense for such an action."[25]

---

[22] Lignum-Vitae Products Corp. and Furniture Workers, 6 *LA* 63 (1946).

[23] The basic arbitration agreement between the Newspaper Publishers Association and the Printing Pressmen prohibits informing the neutral of wage offers made in negotiations. Needless to say, the conduct of the parties in executive session has not always conformed to this rule. See the dissenting opinions in Newspaper Publishers Assn. and Printing Pressmen, 12 *LA* 448 (1949) and the appeal in 13 *LA* 968 (1949).

[24] National Academy of Arbitrators, "Report of Committee on Ethics" (Washington: January 14, 1949), p. 5. Kuhn argues that the inadequacies of the wage criteria give "strong support to the use of a tripartite arbitration board, using a mediation ... approach." Alfred Kuhn, *Arbitration in Transit, an Evaluation of Wage Criteria,* Labor Relations Series (Philadelphia: University of Pennsylvania Press, 1952), p. 181.

[25] Pittsburgh Railways Co. and Amalgamated Street Railway Employees, 14 *LA* 672 (1949). See also the union concurring opinion in Employees' National Conference Committee and Eastern, Western and Southeastern Carriers' Conference Committees, 2 *LA* 286 (1946).

Obviously, compromise can be effectuated more readily under a tripartite than under a unitary arbitration system. The risk that the board will fail to reach a majority decision is ever present; rare instances of impasse have occurred.

These arguments, then, present a persuasive case for a three-way board in wage cases. There is, however, a disadvantage that deserves note. Any accretion in size must carry with it added burdens of expense and administrative inefficiency. Partisan representatives are usually paid for their time; hearings are extended by duplicating questions; more copies of documents must be prepared; time schedules are drawn out. Under some circumstances, therefore, the values of tripartitism are not worth their cost.[26]

The discussion thus far has assumed a simple tripartite structure with a single representative on each side (1-1-1). Numerous variations are possible. In essence, however, they are of two types: those in which the neutrals must have partisan support to render a decision (1-1-1, 1-2-2, 2-2-2, 1-3-3) and those in which the neutrals have final authority (3-1-1 and 1-1-1, in which the submission gives only the public member the vote). For both the substantive and procedural reasons given above there is little ground for deviating from the basic 1-1-1 arrangement in a wage case. On the other hand, when several issues are involved, including at least one that cannot be compromised, a less flexible form may be preferable. The larger boards, of course, suffer from the administrative deficiencies of tripartitism in aggravated form.

A final point concerns the policy of the chairman of a conventional board in face of a voting impasse. Some suggest that he resign when he fails to win a majority.[27] Although this proposal has great appeal to harassed neutrals, it has no merit as a policy in wage cases. In agreeing to serve, the arbitrator enters into an implicit contractual obligation to render an award (in some states the law makes it explicit); by the same token, the parties, in engaging him, assume a duty to comply with his decision. By retiring, therefore, he would repudiate his agreement and thereby undermine the objectives of both collective bargaining and arbitration. Rather than flight, the impasse suggests more imaginative efforts at settlement.

Further, the act of resignation should have an underpinning of high

---

[26] An employer service bulletin adds another qualification, namely, that unions, generally speaking, are more competently represented than management. Hence the shrewd employer should favor a single arbitrator unless he has a topflight spokesman. National Foremen's Institute, Inc., *Pitfalls to Avoid in Labor Arbitration* (Deep River, Conn.: 1946), pp. 7–8.

[27] M. Herbert Syme, "Tripartitism and Compulsory Arbitration" and Emanuel Stein, "Problem Areas in Labor Arbitration," *Proceedings of New York University Third Annual Conference on Labor* (Albany: Bender, 1950), pp. 176, 203.

principle, and it is almost impossible to conceive of a contemporary wage case so based. Is a rate of $1.45 per hour more "moral" than one of $1.50? Or vice versa? There is such a grounding for the solutions to many grievance matters and noneconomic contract cases. However, the moral content has been largely drained out of wages. By quitting, therefore, the arbitrator would be defending nothing beyond his own desire to be left in peace, a right, incidentally, that he had contracted away for a consideration.[28]

5. *Arbitrating Wage Reductions*

The arbitration of employer demands for wage cuts in periods of declining business activity presents special problems not encountered at other times. These stem from the firm resistance of workers and unions to reductions, clearly exceeding that of employers to increases. An example will demonstrate:

Depression fell upon the Philadelphia upholstery industry in 1927, and three years later the employers were demanding a 25 per cent wage cut. The local upholstery workers' union, long established in the market, refused to countenance this proposal. The international, concerned lest the industry collapse along with its members' jobs, successfully forced the local to submit wages to arbitration under an old but never-invoked clause in the contract. A board then awarded a 14 per cent reduction for one season in hope of arresting the flight of the industry from Philadelphia. The local, despite appeals from the parent body, flouted the award by calling a desperation strike which was, in turn, lost.[29] It may be added in the same vein that the disenchantment of the coal and railway unions with wage arbitration arose from related experiences during the depression of 1920–1922.[30]

Under conditions such as those facing the Philadelphia upholstery industry, arbitration can only infrequently serve a useful purpose. David L. Cole has argued that collective bargaining is much preferable to arbitration in wage-cutting, since the parties should assume responsibility for a decision that is intimately theirs.[31] In those few disputes,

---

[28] The *threat* of resignation unaccompanied by its fulfillment, on the other hand, may be a fruitful bargaining tactic to coax out a settlement. The usual wage impasse in a tripartite board, of course, reflects just this kind of tactic by the parties rather than a deep-seated conflict over principle.

[29] Gladys L. Palmer, *Union Tactics and Economic Change* (Philadelphia: University of Pennsylvania Press, 1932), pp. 57–70.

[30] V. W. Lanfear, *Business Fluctuations and the American Labor Movement* (New York: Columbia University Press, 1924), p. 94. See also the dissenting opinion in Bates Mfg. Co. and Textile Workers, 18 *LA* 631 (1952).

[31] "The Wage Reduction Problem in Wage Determinations," *Daily Labor Report*, no. 208, October 22, 1952, p. D-1.

however, in which the decisive union leadership recognizes the necessity for a reduction, this procedure can be very helpful. The inescapable wage cut, in fact, supplies the classic condition for political, or "whipping boy," arbitration.

Between 1916 and 1920, for example, the Chicago job printing industry and the printing trades negotiated seven wage increases based on the rising cost of living. They had, as a matter of fact, established an escalator arrangement with the understanding that wage rates would follow the index. In the last half of 1920, retail prices dropped sharply and the employers demanded a reduction. The union leaders, fearful of membership reaction, sought by delay and other means to escape the escalator agreement. They finally were persuaded to submit the matter to arbitration and the board dutifully administered the cut. The responsibility for a decision they could not avoid was thereby transferred to others.[32]

Arbitration of this sort may be conducted both with and without the prior understanding of the neutral. There is no evidence that the above case included advance briefing of the board. It had no alternative on the merits. A recent wage award affecting a large segment of an important industry entailed, in effect, an implicit arrangement. That is, at the opening of the hearing the union president left no doubt that his demand for an increase was merely for the record. Sometimes, however, there is an explicit agreement at the outset. Dickinson cites such a case:

> In a recent arbitration of the employers' demand for a wage cut, the chief union officials were privately convinced beforehand that the economic position of that branch of their industry demanded some reduction in wages. . . . Through intermediaries a considerable measure of agreement was reached with the employers that such relief could be afforded. . . . To this extent, therefore, the arbitration proceedings were formalities, enabling the leaders of the parties to avoid suspicions that they had "sold out" their constituencies. The neutral arbitrator well understood the position when he accepted; he knew that he would be the most unpopular individual with the rank and file of both sides after the decision; and his decision in the main followed the informal understanding reached before arbitration.
>
> When this decision was handed down, the union officers adopted and published to the membership, a resolution strongly condemning the arbitration award (which doubtless was somewhat more unfavorable to the workers than they had expected)— but insisting that the union should maintain its good reputation by abiding by its agreements, one of which had been to accept the results of this arbitration.[33]

This "whipping boy" conception of arbitration is one of the reasons for the success of the impartial chairmanship set up in 1929 in the full-

---

[32] F. H. Bird, "The Cost of Living as a Factor in Recent Wage Adjustments in the Book and Job Branch of the Chicago Printing Industry," *American Economic Review*, XI (December, 1921), 622–642.

[33] Z. Clark Dickinson, *Collective Wage Determination* (New York: Ronald, 1941), p. 28, n. 11.

fashioned hosiery industry. Both parties at that time recognized that wage cuts were inevitable and called in an outsider to whom they could shift the onus of decision-making. The hosiery employers and the union, both sophisticated in these matters, soon learned, however, that their permanent arrangement was too valuable in contract administration to be risked in wage cases. As Kennedy reports:

> Decisions in this area are very likely to make the arbitrator *persona non grata* to one or both of the parties. . . . No matter what decision the arbitrator makes in a general wage-level case, therefore, one or both of the parties are likely to feel that the decision is grossly inequitable, especially when conditions necessitate a general decrease in wages. Since employees are usually working only part time and are having difficulty making ends meet at the existing wage rates, they find it difficult to accept even a small wage cut; and since manufacturers are usually suffering severe losses at such times, they find it difficult to regard even a sizable wage cut as adequate. . . . The feeling against an arbitrator after a decision of this type in one or both of the groups may be so general and so severe that the one decision destroys his usefulness to the industry. It is significant in this respect that of the six arbitrators who have been chosen to determine general wage-level changes under the flexibility clause in the hosiery industry, not one has been invited to serve a second time.[34]

The hosiery case suggests two of the conditions that induce the political arbitration of wage cuts, namely, a mature collective relationship and incomplete unionization of the industry. With respect to the first, more innocent parties would either be unaware of the possibilities of arbitration for this purpose or would be fearful of trusting an outsider with so vital a matter. Obviously, the employer must be willing to assist in saving face for the union leadership if arbitration is to occur at all. Second, if the union controlled the whole industry, the likelihood is remote that it would be a party to a reduction under any circumstances. In face of pressure of wage-cutting by nonunion employers in an industry with intense price competition in the product market, however, a union is left with the unhappy alternative of accepting lower wages or of losing the jobs of its members. Union leaders have little choice but to accept the reduction to preserve their organization. Hence arbitration can serve to anaesthetize the patient while surgery is carried out.

The arbitration of wage reductions is further complicated with respect to criteria. As has been pointed out, standards of wage determination leave much to be desired on the upside; their inadequacies are particularly glaring in wage-cutting.

The employer, of course, is the activating party in insisting upon lower wages. This is normally based upon an exclusive concern with his own financial condition. Such factors as reduced competitive prices,

---

[34] Thomas Kennedy, *Effective Labor Arbitration* (Philadelphia: University of Pennsylvania Press, 1948), pp. 37–38.

a smaller market, diminishing financial reserves, and narrower profit margins cause him to seek cost savings, of which wages may comprise a significant element. These conditions may be patent, demonstrable, and persuasive; their translation into a reduction in wage rates, however, is fraught with difficulty.

The effect that a given wage cut will have upon sales, prices, profits, and employment is in the area of the imponderable and immeasurable. Neither the parties nor the arbitrator are competent to equate these results in monetary wage rates. Further, such a calculation necessitates prediction rather than analysis of fact, since the most important considerations evoke the future rather than the past. Few arbitrators are descended from gypsy fortune tellers. Finally, the "badness" of business is not precisely convertible into cents per hour. Wagewise, for example, is the employer's condition five cents or ten cents "bad"?[85]

These inadequacies are illustrated by a series of arbitrations in 1920–1922 involving the New York Employing Printers Association and the printing trades. The parties disagreed sharply over the financial condition of the industry. In the first case, the employers refused to open their books and the arbitrators, accordingly, ignored their plea of inability to pay. In the second, the Association submitted its own accountant's report. The board, after subjecting him to searching examination, ignored his data because their confidence in them was shattered. In the last proceeding, each party selected an accountant and the two together drew up a plan for a survey and chose a third accountant to make it. He examined the books of those concerns with usable data and prepared consolidated figures. The first two accountants then wrote a joint report on the financial state of the industry.

The procedure, no doubt, was impeccably impartial. The parties, however, disagreed sharply on the results. The unions demanded dollar figures, while the Association insisted on per cent of change. The employers attacked the results as being unrepresentative of the industry as a whole. Only forty-eight of the seven hundred firms in the city were included, and they were said to be the most profitable ones. The unions countered that these forty-eight were typical of the two hundred members of the Association and were, in any case, the only ones whose books were usable. In the face of this controversy, the arbitrators ignored the report and based the wage change solely on the cost of living.[86]

This suggests that cost of living sometimes provides the arbitrator with a more precise guide for cutting wages. That was certainly the case in 1920–1922, when retail prices broke sharply with general business

[85] The problems of applying this criterion are discussed at length on pp. 77–90.
[86] Soule, *op. cit.,* pp. 25–26, 41, 63, 85–94.

activity and many, probably most, downward wage awards were hinged to them. The relationship between consumer prices and the financial condition of the firm, however, is far from automatic. In the mild recession of 1949, for example, the sales of concerns in such industries as textiles and shoes declined much more rapidly than the BLS index. Although a full discussion would lead us far afield, it is probably safe to suggest that the relationship of 1920–1922 will not again prevail. In this context, the Consumers' Price Index can serve only as the crudest kind of measuring rod for wage reduction.

Much the same may be said of comparisons. They, of course, provide a precise guide to wage decisions but are more workable on the up than on the down side. As unions approach complete organization over industries, the likelihood of uncovering intraindustry wage reductions for comparative purposes becomes decreasingly likely. Furthermore, interindustry comparisons are less persuasive.

6. *The Rigged Case*

The discussion of wage-cutting suggests the more general problem of the "rigged case." By this is meant the arbitration the result of which is known in advance to union, employer, and arbitrator. Its purpose, of course, is to save face for leaders on either or both sides. The arbitrator's face, in Shulman's phrase, is expendable. An essential element of the rigged case is secrecy; that is, persons interested in the outcome (union members, local union leaders, segments of an employers' association) have no knowledge of the prearranged agreement.

As a consequence, it is not possible to determine how widespread rigging is. The published award affords no clue, since it is specifically written not to read like a predetermined decision. Collecting rigged arbitrations, therefore, presents much the same obstacles as taking a census of undercover agents. This much, at least, can be said: it occurs with some frequency in the hosiery, textile, garment, clothing, and shoe and leather industries. Moreover, in companies that have piece-rate systems and work-loads rigging is often used in grievance cases.

The use of this device is a sign of division within the union or employers' association. There may be a split between international and local or between leadership and membership over wage policy. Or there may be disagreement between high cost and low cost producers within an association. A rigged arbitration provides a formula by which the dominant element may obtain the terms it regards as necessary without assuming formal responsibility for doing so.

Proponents of the judicial interpretation of arbitration find rigging repugnant. Its justification stems from a bargaining view of this process.

If industrial harmony is accepted as a prime objective of arbitration, the predetermined award acquits itself as a pragmatic means of achieving this goal. A deal between the Amalgamated Clothing Workers, the New York clothing manufacturers, and an arbitration board in 1919, for example, terminated a work stoppage and gave both sides the terms they really wanted. In the words of Professor Ripley, the chairman of the board, "that [agreement] ended the strike except for the slight matter of detail of enduring several thousand pages of an official record."[37]

The rigged case requires an arbitrator willing to serve under these conditions. Although some neutrals refuse to do so, there is no doubt that many accept them. This is, generally speaking, not a sign of lack of integrity, but rather of a desire to foster the ends of collective bargaining. The arbitrator, however, must assure himself at the outset that the substantive result he is used for is one in which he concurs. He must either know the principals well enough to be certain of their good faith or he must conduct a preliminary investigation to certify this knowledge. In a recent case, for example, an employers' association and a dominated labor organization requested an arbitrator of standing to award a prearranged wage cut. On the basis of his familiarity with the relationship and with the economics of the industry, he refused to accept the case. The neutral's standard should be whether the rigged result approximates the award he would have come up with in a good-faith proceeding. As Stein has pointed out, "If the arbitrator is certain that the 'deal' is legitimate and represents the result of genuine arms-length bargaining between the parties, there would appear to be sound reasons for his participation."[38]

A tripartite board is the appropriate structural form for the rigged wage case. This is, in part, because wage changes in general are not well adapted to one-man arbitration. More important, however, is the usefulness of a tripartite arrangement in supporting the masquerade through the dissenting opinion. By his dissent a partisan board member can give the appearance of striving valiantly in the interests of his constituents against insuperable odds. These opinions make impressive reading in union newspapers and employers' association newsletters.

With these remarks, we close the discussion of those procedural problems peculiar to the arbitration of wages. This leads us to the basic substantive matter, the criteria of wage determination.

---

[37] Quoted in George Soule, *Sidney Hillman* (New York: Macmillan, 1939), p. 196.
[38] Stein, *op. cit.*, p. 182.

IV. CRITERIA OF WAGE DETERMINATION: I

THIS CHAPTER and the one that follows are concerned with the criteria of wage determination and deal basically with the arguments of unions and employers and the decisions of arbitrators as they illuminate these factors in actual cases. The reports constitute a workable empirical tool —perhaps the best that can be found—for their analysis. This stems from the presumptive rationality of wage arbitration, a condition that not even the innocent would exact of negotiations. The inescapable necessity to present and weigh evidence in arbitration requires an elaborate formal consideration of criteria. This, in turn, pays an incidental dividend to scholarship.

Before turning systematically to the standards, it is necessary to establish certain qualifying generalizations: the parties' goal of victory rather than of principle, criteria as rationalization and not as reason, and the immeasurability of bargaining power in the awards. After disposing of these preliminaries, the remainder of this chapter considers the most important of the wage standards, namely, comparisons. The succeeding chapter discusses the other criteria.

1. Some Qualifications

Like medical diagnoses, arbitration awards deal with imagined as well as with real symptoms. Since the patient and the doctor may not be able to distinguish between fact and fancy, it follows that the reader of the latter's report is no better off. This is often of little consequence because the conjured may be as serious as the incontrovertible ailment. This is a roundabout way of saying that an arbitration award cannot always be taken on its face. To change the image, the legal tender of the printed page may be bogus money to the parties. There is, unfortunately, no simple device to uncover hidden forces behind a particular written award. These factors, however, are fairly well known in general, and should be stated at the outset by way of qualification.

The primary goal of both sides in wage arbitration is victory measured in cents per hour rather than justice. The union insists upon an increase of x cents and the company is willing to pay no more than y cents. The establishment of "principles" of wage determination may be of incidental value in achieving this aim, or it may be of no moment, or it may even be an embarrassment. "Our primary goal," a business agent has said, "is an ever improving standard of living for our workers."[1] Such a program, consistently pursued, would soon leave a nice structure of wage criteria in ruins.

---

[1] Quoted in W. S. Woytinsky and Associates, *Labor and Management Look at Collective Bargaining* (New York: Twentieth Century Fund, 1949), p. 75.

For unions and management, then, standards of wage determination often constitute the rationalizations to justify rather than the reasons for reaching positions. Criteria sometimes serve no other purpose than to drape a cloak of respectability about the shoulders of a predetermined policy. The parties, for example, are notoriously inconsistent in the factors they cite, particularly with reference to the business cycle. In good times unions urge and employers ignore cost of living; in bad times these arguments are turned about. Some companies refuse to open their books; others insist upon doing so. Illustrations are legion and there is no need further to labor the obvious.

This unblushingly sensible opportunism is not confined to the parties. Arbitrators, too, engage in rationalization. The historian of the Kansas Industrial Court reports:

> The best it did, and for that matter the best it could have done, was to arrive at what appeared to be a conclusion acceptable to both parties and then to dress this up in high-sounding legal phrases. The judges did not labor long under the delusion that in wage cases they were meting out justice to all parties concerned.[2]

In defense, a learned committee of arbitrators points out that "criticism of awards in this area of arbitration [wages] depends very often on whose ox is being gored."[3]

At this low point of cynicism it might seem the wise course to give up any serious analysis of criteria as hopeless. To do so, however, would be like tossing away a shovel because it was a slow tool for leveling the top of a hill. In the absence of a bulldozer, it might be the best implement available. Hills must be cleared, and the conventional standards are the only tools at hand. As Feis has observed:

> Most principles of wage settlement originated as logical defenses of private purposes or desires—as is commonly the case with principles now used to regulate human relationships. Their possible value may be none the less on account of their origin; private purposes and desires may well be just as unjust, practicable as impracticable.[4]

A final word of qualification must be said concerning the unseen and immeasurable but, nevertheless, vital criterion of bargaining power. No union or employer argues and, certainly, no arbitrator decides that an award should be based on the parties' relative strength.[5] That it is a key consideration was pointed out long ago:

> Voluntary arbitration . . . is often neither more nor less than the victory of the stronger over the weaker party to the contest; that is to say, the decision is frequently

---

[2] Domenico Gagliardo, *The Kansas Industrial Court* (Lawrence: University of Kansas Press, 1941), p. 235.

[3] National Academy of Arbitrators, "Report of Committee on Ethics" (Washington: January 14, 1949), p. 5.

[4] Herbert Feis, *Principles of Wage Settlement* (New York: Wilson, 1924), p. 10.

[5] The exception to prove this rule is in San Diego Retail Grocery Industry and Retail Clerks, 11 *LA* 880 (1948).

given to the side that would have won, and in proportion to what it would have won, had the issue not been submitted to arbitration, but been fought to the end through a strike or lockout.[6]

This view is, doubtless, overstated for the simple reason that bargaining power is not susceptible to precise translation into cents per hour. In very general terms, however, it is of signal importance in many wage arbitrations, even though it does not appear in the reports.

With these qualifications established, we may now turn to the formal criteria, beginning, of course, with comparisons.

2. *Comparisons*

For the reader who has traveled with us from the outset, the central importance of comparisons in wage determination needs no reëmphasis. "The most powerful influence," Ross observes, "linking together separate wage bargains into an interdependent system is the force of equitable comparison."[7] This consideration justifies a brief discussion of emulative behavior in general.

The writer who has dug to the roots of this problem, of course, is Veblen. He points out that "the propensity for emulation—for invidious comparison—is of ancient growth and is a pervading trait of human nature." In a pecuniary society such as ours, relative success is measured by monetary status. Hence the "accepted legitimate end of effort becomes the achievement of a favourable comparison with other men." This propensity to emulate cannot be satiated; the goal is ever-retreating. The aim of the individual is to attain parity with those with whom he is accustomed to class himself. When that is achieved, he lifts his sights to a new and higher level. "The standard of expenditure . . . is an ideal of consumption that lies beyond our reach." The worker's cry for "more" (like that of his boss) is never fulfilled.[8]

---

[6] John Mitchell, *Organized Labor* (Philadelphia: American Book and Bible House, 1903), p. 338. See also Thomas L. Norton, *Trade-Union Policies in the Massachusetts Shoe Industry, 1919–1929* (New York: Columbia University Press, 1932), p. 359, and James F. Bogardus, *Industrial Arbitration in the Book and Job Printing Industry of New York City* (Philadelphia: University of Pennsylvania Press, 1934), p. 76.

[7] Arthur M. Ross, *Trade Union Wage Policy* (Berkeley: University of California Press, 1948), p. 6.

[8] Thorstein Veblen, *The Theory of the Leisure Class* (New York: Modern Library, 1934), *passim*. The insatiable capacity of the comparison is illustrated by the employer dissent in the *Berkshire Street Railway* case: "Apparently the Chairman believes that 'inequality' between the employees of these two companies with common ownership has been eliminated. Nothing could be further from the fact. What has been done creates a new inequity, or at least this will unquestionably be the claim of New England Transportation Company operators. . . . To their mind elimination of the differential will doubtless be considered an inequity. So, all that the Chairman has done has been to 'remove' one inequity by creating another; Peter has been robbed to pay Paul." Berkshire Street Railway Co. and Amalgamated Street Railway Employees, 10 *LA* 139 (1948).

The quest for parity is a defense against derogation. "The passion for equality," Hoffer observes, "is partly a passion for anonymity; to be one thread of the many which make up a tunic; one thread not distinguishable from the others. No one can then point us out; measure us against others to expose our inferiority."[9] In wages, as in other areas of behavior, individuals and social organizations seek to guard themselves against an indictment for failure by achieving and maintaining parity with their peers.

Comparisons are preëminent in wage determination because all parties at interest derive benefit from them. To the worker they permit a decision on the adequacy of his income. He feels no discrimination if he stays abreast of other workers in his industry, his locality, his neighborhood. They are vital to the union because they provide guidance to its officials upon what must be insisted upon and a yardstick for measuring their bargaining skill. In the presence of internal factionalism or rival unionism, the power of comparisons is enhanced. The employer is drawn to them because they assure him that competitors will not gain a wage-cost advantage and that he will be able to recruit in the local labor market. Small firms (and unions) profit administratively by accepting a ready-made solution; they avoid the expenditure of time and money needed for working one out themselves. Arbitrators benefit no less from comparisons. They have "the appeal of precedent and . . . awards based thereon are apt to satisfy the normal expectations of the parties and to appear just to the public."[10]

This appearance of justice satisfies a universal aim. All the world favors a "fair" wage. Yet, how is it to be determined? There is, obviously, no absolute answer to this question. The pragmatic solution resides in the comparison, which "seems to offer a presumptive test of the fairness of a wage."[11] The rate that satisfies the test of comparison, if not "fair," is, at least, not "unfair."

A further attraction of comparisons is ready translatability into cents per hour. Most standards of wage determination present some and often insuperable difficulties on this score. How, for example, does one convert a firm's unfavorable business outlook into an exact set of lower wage rates? Or, assuming the validity of the consumer-purchasing-power theory, precisely how much does one raise wages in a particular bargaining unit in order to create full employment in the economy as a whole? There are no such hurdles of calculation to leap in the case of comparisons. If comparable firm x grants a cents, firm y simply ac-

---

[9] Eric Hoffer, *The True Believer* (New York: Harper, 1951), pp. 31–32.

[10] Note, "Factors Relied on by Arbitrators in Determining Wage Rates," *Columbia Law Review*, XLVII (September, 1947), 1028.

[11] Feis, *op. cit.*, p. 339.

cepts the same amount. As Kerr has noted, the comparison "provides a precise, objective figure, rather than an artificially contrived rate."[12] Ross adds: "The ready-made settlement supplies an answer, a solution, a formula."[13]

This suggests another pragmatic attraction of comparisons: they are easily understood by everyone. The management of firm *y*, its employees, the union officials, and the arbitrator need little power of analysis to grasp the significance of *a* cents per hour. There is, moreover, no need to look behind the action of firm *x* to evaluate the validity of that amount (it may be entirely spurious). Wage decision *a* is simply accepted on its face. Most other criteria do not so neatly side-step the distress of intellectual effort.[14]

There is one type of wage decision for which comparisons provide no guidance: the first one. Obviously, there must be a basis for comparison and the wage leader (Dunlop refers to this situation as "the key bargain") has none. The pace-setter must, therefore, make the determination on other grounds. An arbitrator's denial of an increase to a very high-paid group, for example, led to this union dissent:

> To conclude that these employees are not entitled to a wage increase simply because they are receiving top wages would give recognition to the principle that all wage earners who have attained the wage ceiling for their respective classifications can never expect another wage increase unless they resort to strike action to enforce their demands.[15]

These remarks suggest that arbitration is not well adapted to the wage leadership dispute. The institutional discussion in chapter ii confirms the fact that the parties concur in this view.[16] The "key bargain," however, plays a leading role in collective bargaining; to discuss that here would lead us far afield.

A further qualification stems from the assumption of an average in basing wage decisions on comparisons. Deviations in either direction tend to be carried along by the pervasive force of the standard. The low-profit firm, for example, may be hurt, while one at the other end of the scale may benefit. That is, by its evenhandedness the comparison disregards individual differences.

---

[12] Pacific Gas & Electric Co. and Utility Workers, 7 *LA* 534 (1947).

[13] Ross, *op. cit.*, p. 52.

[14] Hoffer adds: "Imitation is often a shortcut to a solution. We copy when we lack the inclination, the ability or the time to work out an independent solution. People in a hurry will imitate more readily than people at leisure. Hustling thus tends to produce uniformity." *Op. cit.*, p. 101.

[15] United Press Assns. and Commercial Telegraphers, 14 *LA* 868 (1950).

[16] Dunlop has suggested that the arbitrator ask at the outset: "Is the rate on the property recognized as a 'key bargain'? If so, the relation to other rates in the industry may be expected generally to be less significant." Twin City Rapid Transit Co. and Amalgamated Street Railway Employees, 10 *LA* 590 (1948).

In the discussion that follows, comparisons are classified into the following structural subgroups: (1) intraindustry, (2) interindustry, (3) intracompany, (4) intraunion, and (5) interunion. The first three are based on an arrangement of the firm, the remaining two of the union. Any taxonomical system is inherently arbitrary and must approach the zone of half-truth. No particular brief is held for this one; it is simply more workable than its alternatives. An obvious difficulty is the overlapping of firm and union forms. That is, an intraindustry may be at the same time an intraunion comparison. The parties and arbitrators normally use the employer rather than the labor organization as the basis for comparison. That fact is recognized in the present discussion.

Methods of calculation vary around the constant substantive principle of the comparison. The present classification system is cast in terms of the latter, and properly so, although the problems of administering comparisons will sometimes involve the computing technique. Among the more common ways to calculate are the following: (1) wage levels, that is, average hourly earnings of all employees in the unit; (2) rates, necessarily important under craft unionism; (3) a key rate considered representative of the whole operation, for example, the one-man operator rate in transit; and (4) base rates under incentive systems. In the majority of cases the parties have long since resolved the problem of calculation. Only occasionally, therefore, does the arbitrator have to square off against it as a disputed issue.

a. *Intraindustry comparisons.* The intraindustry comparison is more commonly cited than any other form of comparison, or, for that matter, any other criterion. More important, the weight it receives is clearly preëminent; it leads by a wide margin in the first rankings of arbitrators.[17] Hence there is no risk in concluding that it is of paramount importance among the wage-determining standards.

Wage parity within the industry is so compelling to arbitrators that, absent qualifications dealt with below, they invariably succumb to its force. Its persuasiveness, in fact, provides as sound a basis for prediction as may be uncovered in social affairs.[18] The loyalty of arbitrators to this criterion at the general level could be documented at length; a few examples will suffice. In the award that terminated the great 1946 maritime strike, Fly wrote:

The cessation of shipping has brought paralysis to the waterborne coastwise and foreign commerce of the nation. . . . The public interest demands that this state of

---

[17] See figure 2, above.

[18] A sophisticated union leader has stated: "We would try to get arbitration if we were apart on wages; and if it were an established fact that other things prevailed in the industry, we would try to insist on arbitration." Cited in Woytinsky, *op. cit.,* p. 58.

paralysis in the maritime industry be alleviated promptly. It is of primary importance that the whole scheme of inequities giving rise to this condition be wiped out. Stability, so fundamental to the nation's economy, is but a will-of-the-wisp where men are called upon to do the same work at different rates of pay. The effort of the arbitrator here and in companion cases is therefore to achieve the greatest possible degree of uniformity in pay and important working conditions.

The principle of equal pay for equal work has become a fixed part of public policy. . . . The maritime industry has long been plagued by the presence of wage inequities. . . . Whatever historical explanations may be for the origins of these wage inequities, they cannot be attributed to reasonable wage differentials existing by virtue of separate labor-market areas, distinguishable job duties, etc. By and large, they are traceable simply to the presence of long-standing wage inequities which to a real extent have only been aggravated by recent unequal wage increases.[19]

A case of classic simplicity is that involving the *Newark Call.* There were two Sunday papers in the town, the *Call* and the *Ledger,* which had had a related wage history. The Newspaper Guild, however, asked that a differential in favor of the former's employees should be created. The arbitrator replied: "Such a practically stabilized situation, involving two competing papers in the same labor market area and covering the same territory, should not be disturbed, to the advantage of one newspaper and the disadvantage of the other, except on grounds which are extremely compelling."[20]

The principle of intraindustry rate parity is long-standing. Before World War I, arbitrators were virtually unanimous in awarding system-wide uniformity of rates for the same type of railroad service. Similarly, Kennedy reports that the leading "common law" principle evolved since 1929 by the Impartial Chairmanship in the hosiery industry is identical piece rates for the same product on similar equipment in all the mills of the Manufacturers Association.[21]

A corollary of the preëminence of the intraindustry comparison is the superior weight it wins when found in conflict with another standard of wage determination. The balancing of opposing factors, of course, is central in the arbitration function, and most commonly arises in the present context over an employer argument of financial adversity.

A classic case is the Australian award of 1909 involving the Broken Hill Proprietary Company. The miners' union had negotiated a uniform scale covering the operations at Broken Hill, excepting this large

---

[19] Atlantic & Gulf Coast Shippers and Maritime Union, 4 *LA* 468–469 (1946).

[20] *Newark Call* and Newspaper Guild, 3 *LA* 320–321 (1946). For other general statements see Fifth Ave. Coach Co. and Transport Workers, 4 *LA* 548 (1946); Committee for Tanker Cos. and Marine Engineers, 12 *LA* 855 (1949); Pittsburgh Railways Co. and Amalgamated Street Railway Employees, 14 *LA* 662 (1949).

[21] J. Noble Stockett, Jr., *The Arbitral Determination of Railway Wages* (Boston: Houghton Mifflin, 1918), pp. 8–9; Thomas Kennedy, *Effective Labor Arbitration* (Philadelphia: University of Pennsylvania Press, 1948), p. 172.

firm, and based its claim upon the intraindustry comparison. The company, however, pointed to the uncontroverted fact that, at the current rate of extraction, ore would be exhausted in five years and would be uneconomic to mine in two and a half. Without a favorable wage differential, it would shortly be compelled to go out of business. The Arbitration Court dismissed this contention and held wage parity the paramount factor. Although the end of operations would be a catastrophe, it was inevitable in any case. The basic cause lay in the exhaustion of the ore rather than in the scale. "It is not for the Court to dictate to employers what work they should carry on. It can merely ... prescribe fit conditions for human labour, if the Company employs it."[22]

The Kansas City transit case of 1947 presented a similar problem. The company had suffered a quarter-century of financial hardship, including several receiverships, and desperately needed new equipment. There was no cash reserve, a fact confirmed by an invitation to the employees to audit the books. The arbitrator, nevertheless, awarded a fifteen-cent wage increase, approximately the amount granted at the two most comparable properties, St. Louis and the Twin Cities.[23]

The Wisconsin electric coöperative case of 1950 entailed a related and more challenging issue. The Dairyland Power Cooperative was generally regarded as the bellwether of the rural electrification movement. Its function was to supply power to farmers whose location rendered them unprofitable prospects for the private utilities. "A significant social purpose was thus served," the arbitration board observed. "Not only the farmers, but the economy as a whole benefited." Dairyland, however, was inherently a high-cost operation. Widely-spaced consumers required large construction outlays for distribution. More important was the uneven demand of dairy farmers as contrasted with urban customers. The former concentrated the power load in the evening hours, necessitating a plant potential far in excess of what could be used at other times. Finally, Dairyland felt constrained to charge lower rates than its competition to justify itself as a coöperative.

On the other hand, the Electrical Workers insisted upon a comparison with the privately-owned Northern States Power Company. The two operations served the same general area and had similar investments. Employees of both lived in the same communities and had identical jobs. Yet, Northern States wage rates were substantially higher. Here the board faced not only a plea of financial difficulty but also the force of a laudable social objective. Despite these considerations, "the Board

---

[22] Cited in Feis, *op. cit.*, pp. 96–103.
[23] Kansas City Public Service Co. and Amalgamated Street Railway Employees, 8 *LA* 149 (1947).

believes that Cooperative can make no valid claim to special wage treatment. . . . Wages, like materials, are a cost of doing business and Dairyland must pay the fair market price." The award, therefore, narrowed the differential with Northern States.[24]

A conflict between intraindustry comparisons and other criteria appears to arise less frequently. In the 1949 dispute involving Atlantic Coast tanker companies, however, the employers argued for a wage cut based upon a modest drop in the cost of living. The Marine Engineers countered by citing a 1.56 per cent increase granted by dry-cargo operators. Tanker- and dry-cargo adjustments had been identical as to amount in the four preceding general wage changes. Awarding in favor of the union, Livingston wrote: "The principle of parity has been the keystone of the present stability in the maritime industry. The slight decline in the Consumer Price Index would not seem to warrant disturbing that principle."[25]

The force of the intraindustry comparison is inapplicable, because irrelevant, to two situations: industry-wide bargaining and the wage leader. When all the firms in an industry bargain jointly, there is, obviously, no one to follow. The national bargaining structure on the railroads has had this effect in wage determination.[26]

The reason for the inapplicability of the intraindustry comparison to the wage leader has already been suggested.[27] The 1949 Fall River and New Bedford textile arbitration is illustrative. The arbitrator pointed out that this settlement had had a determinative influence upon wage changes in cotton textiles in both the North and other areas in the past. Hence rates paid elsewhere in the industry were of no help in reaching a decision.[28] Dunlop has generalized the origin of the problem in these terms:

A study of wage movements in almost any industry reveals that there are a limited number of "key bargains" which tend to condition the change in wage levels in the industry. These bargains may be described as "growth points" in the wage structure.

[24] Dairyland Power Coop. and Brotherhood of Electrical Workers, 14 *LA* 737, 741 (1950). For other illustrations of the priority given intraindustry comparisons over financial adversity, see Fifth Ave. Coach Co. and Transport Workers, 4 *LA* 548 (1946); Watson Elevator Co. and United Electrical Workers, 8 *LA* 386 (1947); Capital Transit Co. and Amalgamated Street Railway Employees, 9 *LA* 666 (1947). Stockett reports that pre-World War I railway arbitration boards generally applied rate standardization in the face of a plea of inability to pay. *Op. cit.*, p. 29.
[25] Committee for Tanker Cos. and Marine Engineers, 12 *LA* 859 (1949).
[26] Frederic Meyers, "Criteria in the Making of Wage Decisions by 'Neutrals': The Railroads as a Case Study," *Industrial and Labor Relations Review*, IV (April, 1951), 346.
[27] See p. 55, above.
[28] Fall River Textile Mfrs. Assn. and Textile Workers, 11 *LA* 984 (1949).

When wage rates have been fixed on these properties, the rest of the industry tends to adapt itself. . . . All parties in the industry tend to watch these bargains as indicators of the direction and amounts of wage change "in the air."[29]

The decisive criterion in the case of the wage leader must be something other than the intraindustry comparison. David L. Cole has suggested that this vacuum be filled with the interindustry comparison.[30]

The discussion to this point has revealed unanimity of arbitral opinion on the force of the intraindustry comparison with the obvious exceptions of industry-wide bargaining and the wage leader. Agreement at the level of principle is not hard to come by; the critical test arises in applying it to the case-by-case solution of disputes. In the administration of the intraindustry comparison, as might be expected, this happy unanimity evaporates. At bottom, the issues revolve about comparability: are both *a* and *b* really apples? Given the complexities of the American economy, it is almost always possible to stress differences over similarities. For the arbitrator, therefore, the usual question is not whether to recognize the weight of the intraindustry comparison but rather whether to apply it to the facts before him.

In making a determination on comparability, four problems stem from the firm: the borders of the industry, the geographical limits of rate relationships, the significance of ownership and operation, and the nature of the product market.

Industrial classifications are innately arbitrary and, therefore, inevitably provoke controversy at their edges. Among the more common problems in wage determination are the following:

(1) overlapping at the borders of two industries (is fabricating at the site of construction manufacturing or building?)

(2) subindustries (is manufacture of down pillows part of textiles?)

(3) the firm with diverse operations (is General Motors in the automotive, electrical, locomotive, or aircraft industries?)

(4) new industries (is the production of films for television part of motion pictures?)

(5) auxiliary units (are power plants, laboratories, etc. in the industry whose manufacturing operations they support?)

(6) unique firms (in what industry is a company that refines, semifabricates, and fabricates precious metals and manufactures and assembles small instruments and electromechanical assemblies?)

---

[29] Twin City Rapid Transit Co. and Amalgamated Street Railway Employees, 10 *LA* 589 (1948).

[30] R. H. Macy & Co. and Retail, Wholesale and Department Store Union, 11 *LA* 450 (1948).

Obviously, there is no ready formula to resolve these questions. In actual cases, they range in difficulty from those that reasonable men would agree upon to the unanswerable. To the union or management whose goal is victory, an argument of industrial noncomparability may be pure dissimulation. Or the problems may be validly insurmountable. Two rules offer limited guidance to the arbitrator. The first is to decide only upon an appraisal of all the facts. The second is to balance this factor with others that may be of greater significance for the purpose of fixing wages.

A few cases shed light on these problems. In 1946, the rubber industry settled on a general increase of eighteen and a half cents, while the shoe industry granted eight cents. The Rubber Workers, representing employees of the rubber heel division of International Shoe Company, argued that the operation was part of their industry and so due the higher amount. The arbitrator, however, ruled the contrary because the plant was integrated into a shoe manufacturing complex with a "captive" market, there was no historic wage relationship with rubber, and a parallel case had gone against this union.[31]

In a dispute involving a pillow manufacturer the Textile Workers urged his classification within the textile industry. The arbitrator disagreed. The company merely processed feathers and filled ticking; it did not weave yarn into cloth. The only relationship, in fact, was the common bargaining agent. "An analogous case might be to classify a bus line as a railroad because the line was organized by the Brotherhood of Railroad Trainmen."[32]

In a final example, a narrow fabrics operation shared premises with a dye house. The company urged the textile pattern, including a substantial part of narrow fabrics (eight cents), while the union argued for the amount granted in dyeing (twelve and a half cents). The arbitrator held for the former because both the operations and the wage history of narrow fabrics and dye houses were distinct.[33]

These and other cases suggest several tentative conclusions. The first is that the union is often the aggressive party in seeking to define the industry as coterminous with its effective jurisdiction. The other is that the arbitrator frequently gives as much or more weight to wage history as he does to the content of operations.

A related difficulty of administration is the geographical scope of the intraindustry comparison. Very generally speaking, interregional differentials, though still important, have been narrowing in recent years.

---

[31] International Shoe Co. and Rubber Workers, 4 *LA* 733 (1946). See also Aliquippa & Southern Railroad Co. and Railroad Workers, 16 *LA* 539 (1951).
[32] Northern Feather Works and Textile Workers, 9 *LA* 782 (1948).
[33] Heywood Narrow Fabrics and Textile Workers, 6 *LA* 14 (1946).

At the same time, metropolitan rates have been migrating into suburbia and satellite communities. The geography of wage interrelationships, of course, varies from industry to industry. In basic steel, for example, the area for comparison is the nation; for building laborers, on the other hand, it is the locality. These statements are too broad to offer significant guidance to the arbitrator with a tough case to decide. An analysis of the awards, particularly those in transit, where the issue of geography is common, suggests some tentative solutions.

A basic question is whether greater weight should be attached to rates paid by the industry in the locality (or area) than to those paid nationally (or in a distant area). Arbitrators, with the exceptions noted below, are more readily persuaded by proximity than by remoteness. In the 1947 *Twin City Rapid Transit* case, the board observed:

> Prime consideration should be given to agreements voluntarily reached in comparable properties in the general area. For example, wages and conditions in Milwaukee, the city of comparable size nearest geographically to Minneapolis and St. Paul, whose transit company is neither bankrupt, municipally owned, nor municipally supported, might reasonably have ... greater weight ... than Cleveland or Detroit, both municipally owned and farther distant, or Omaha and Council Bluffs, more distant in miles and smaller in population. Smaller and larger cities, however, and cities in other geographical areas should have secondary consideration, for they disclose trends. . . .[34]

When the traditional basis for comparison is something other than nearby rates, arbitrators sometimes temper their awards with local considerations. In the street railway industry, wage changes frequently stem from comparisons with other communities of the same size in the nation. In the 1947 Atlanta case, the arbitrator decided that twenty cents should be granted on this ground. He deducted a nickel, however, because "rates in the South have tended to be somewhat lower than rates nationally, and this factor, although it is of increasingly less importance each year, should be considered as part of the picture."[35] Comparison by size of city, where firmly established as a practice, may completely outweigh local rates. In the 1947 Washington transit case, the arbitrator rejected the employer's urging to consider wages in the area and made his comparison, as the parties had in the past, with cities over a million in population.[36]

---

[34] Twin City Rapid Transit Co. and Amalgamated Street Railway Employees, 7 *LA* 848 (1947). See also Reading Street Railway Co. and Amalgamated Street Railway Employees, 6 *LA* 860 (1947); Green Bus Lines and Amalgamated Street Railway Employees, 8 *LA* 468 (1947); Jamaica Buses and Transport Workers, 4 *LA* 225 (1946); Committee for Tanker Cos. and Marine Engineers, 12 *LA* 855 (1949).

[35] Georgia Power Co. and Amalgamated Street Railway Employees, 8 *LA* 694 (1947).

[36] Capital Transit Co. and Amalgamated Street Railway Employees, 9 *LA* 666 (1947).

This, once again, suggests the force of wage history. Arbitrators are normally under pressure to comply with a standard of comparison evolved by the parties and practiced for years in the face of an effort to remove or create a differential. When Newark milk company engineers asked for a higher rate than that in New York City, the arbitrator rejected the claim with these words: "Where there is, as here, a long history of area rate equalization, only the most compelling reasons can justify a departure from the practice."[37]

The extension of metropolitan rates to outlying areas is, apparently, an exception to this rule. A number of arbitrators have been willing to erase or narrow differentials in satellite cases. In such an award involving the Gary transit system the arbitrator concluded that "the most influential factor in the determination of wage rates in ... outlying suburban towns is the going wage in the metropolis proper [Chicago]."[38]

Competing firms within the same industry often have differing operations with resultant disparity in their wage structures. Hence comparisons between them must be based upon an understanding of these variations. It has been observed, for example, that the Ford Motor Company wage level is not strictly comparable with that of other automobile manufacturers. Ford, unlike the others, makes its own steel; steel rates are high, tending to upend the whole level.[39] An award illustrating this problem is the *Pacific Trailways* case. This bus company served a route directly competitive with Greyhound, a fact suggesting rate parity. The arbitrator, however, noted certain differences: Greyhound's route was more populous and so more productive; its buses were larger; and its drivers moved at a slower pace. These operational deviations, in part, led him to grant less than parity.[40] Generally speaking, operational differences tend to be more important when the basis of calculation is classification rates or average hourly earnings rather than the flat amount of a general wage change.

A similar question arises in the public utilities, particularly transit and power, namely, whether it is proper to compare private with public enterprises. The employer may argue in both directions: either that a private firm suffers disadvantages and is, therefore, entitled to a lower wage, or that a public operation shoulders special burdens that justify

[37] Four Milk Companies and Operating Engineers, 10 *LA* 470 (1948).
[38] Gary Railways and Amalgamated Street Railway Employees, 8 *LA* 642 (1947). See also Safeway Stores and Butchers, 4 *LA* 319 (1946); Crawford Clothes and Retail, Wholesale and Department Store Employees, 5 *LA* 170 (1946).
[39] E. H. Van Delden, "Wage Differentials: Intra- and Inter-Industry," *Proceedings of New York University Third Annual Conference on Labor* (Albany: Bender, 1950), p. 98.
[40] Pacific Trailways and Amalgamated Street Railway Employees, 14 *LA* 111 (1950).

a favorable differential. In the 1946 Washington street railway case, for example, the company objected to comparison with Detroit because the latter's system was municipally owned, was almost wholly exempt from taxation, and operated with a heavy deficit. By contrast, the Dairyland Cooperative has urged that its wages not be compared with a private operation because of the social purposes of the rural electrification movement.[41] The arbitrators gave neither argument decisive weight. The reasoning was set forth in the union's position in the Los Angeles transit case.

> To make such a distinction here [between private and municipal transit properties] would be contrary to the collective bargaining history in the industry and would, in effect, say that employees of municipally operated lines are entitled to a higher wage rate and higher standard of living than employees of privately owned lines and that employees of privately owned lines must assume the financial risk of their employer.[42]

A final administrative issue arising from the employer is the product market. In other words, should the firm at issue be compared only with those with which it competes for sales or with others in related lines as well? Dunlop points out that no other question of comparability is so studded with difficulties, because, excepting the few cases of perfect competition, every business has a specialized clientele.[43] Arbitrators, in the few cases on this point, have given significant weight to the product market. When the union argued for a comparison with rates paid in the industry, generally defined, rather than with those paid by direct competitors, Brissenden observed:

> The American economy once again has become competitive. A firm's ability to survive no longer is, in effect, guaranteed by the Government, as was the case in wartime, at least for firms, like the subject employer, engaged in the metal-working industries. Now it is of crucial importance to such a firm that it be able to maintain at least a rough equivalence of labor and other costs with its competitors. In default of maintenance of such an equivalence, its markets, and the jobs of its workers, will be in jeopardy. The arbitrator concludes, therefore, that little weight can be given to the (rather insubstantial) evidence tending to indicate that some (noncompetitive) employers in the broadly defined electronics industry pay higher wages.[44]

In addition to those difficulties of administering intraindustry comparisons that relate to the employer, there are several which revolve

---

[41] Capital Transit Co. and Amalgamated Street Railway Employees, 1 *LA* 204 (1946); Dairyland Power Coop. and Brotherhood of Electrical Workers, 4 *LA* 431 (1946), 14 *LA* 737 (1950).

[42] Los Angeles Transit Lines and Amalgamated Street Railway Employees, 11 *LA* 124 (1948).

[43] John T. Dunlop, *Collective Bargaining, Principles and Cases* (Chicago: Irwin, 1949), pp. 92–93.

[44] Champion Aero Metal Products and United Electrical Workers, 7 *LA* 283 (1947). See also Heywood Narrow Fabrics and Textile Workers, 6 *LA* 14 (1946).

about the worker. These comparability issues involve the content of jobs, methods of wage payment, regularity of employment, extrarate income ("fringe" benefits), and wage history.

Since the same job titles in different firms often apply to divergent duties, the content of jobs may raise a question of comparability. Dunlop has pointed out that job performance may differ for these reasons: varying ages and types of equipment, differences in the scale of operations, and individualized managerial techniques. He cites by way of example a survey of five customary classifications in forty-seven cotton textile mills. No two firms divided the twenty-five operations performed under these titles in exactly the same way. A comparison of rates "under these circumstances requires a certain amount of temerity."[45] In such a case, clearly, the arbitrator needs both formal job descriptions and the facts of the employees' duties before making a decision. The problem, however, is more acute in the comparison of classification rates and average hourly earnings than in that of across-the-board cents per hour adjustments. This qualification may explain the fact that no cases were found in which job content was a significant issue in the sample of 209 awards.

Variations in methods of wage payment between otherwise comparable firms may impede or prevent a valid comparison. It is extremely difficult, for example, to establish parity between hourly paid and piecework employees. Other complications may intrude as well, such as rate ranges, group incentives, and commissions. A study of industries in which wage uniformity is the bargaining objective revealed at least seven different bases of calculation (unit of output, skill and effort, hours of labor, rate ranges, minimum rates, rate changes, and total costs).[46] Here again, the qualification is primarily important where the comparison is of job rates or of average hourly earnings.[47]

A further hurdle to administering the intraindustry comparison is regularity of employment. Wage differentials are common, for example, between craftsmen employed by utilities or manufacturing firms and those with the same skills who work in the building trades. Their justification lies in differences in the steadiness of employment offered by these industries. The problem is discussed below.[48]

Much the same may be said of nonrate monetary benefits. Such

---

[45] Dunlop, *op. cit.,* p. 89.

[46] Thomas Kennedy, *The Significance of Wage Uniformity,* Industry-Wide Collective Bargaining Series (Philadelphia: University of Pennsylvania Press, 1949), p. 1.

[47] The complexities introduced by differing wage payment methods in even so compact an industry as wool felt is revealed in Felters Co. and Textile Workers, 13 *LA* 702 (1949).

[48] See p. 101.

"fringes" as vacations, holidays, and welfare plans may vary among firms in the same industry and thereby complicate the wage comparison. This question, too, is treated below.[49]

The last of the factors related to the worker is wage history. Judged by the behavior of arbitrators, it is the most significant consideration in administering the intraindustry comparison, since the past wage relationship is commonly used to test the validity of other qualifications.[50] The logic of this position is clear: the ultimate purpose of the arbitrator is to fix wages, not to define the industry, change the method of wage payment, and so on. If he discovers that the parties have historically based wage changes on just this kind of comparison, there is virtually nothing to dissuade him from doing so again.[51] By the same token, if they have not had a wage relationship over time, he is likely to refuse to create one.[52]

A wage history is measurable on two planes: amount and time. Its weight is a direct function of the closeness with which both approach identity. If firms *a* and *b* have made exactly the same cents-per-hour adjustments on exactly the same dates for a number of years, that fact is more impressive than any dilution on either count. Variations, however, are often deceptive, suggesting the advisability of looking beneath the surface. For example, the cost to an employer of a particular rate increase granted by others in the industry may be, in part, converted into an additional holiday. Or, in an industry dominated by a large firm, small employers may delay before putting the same wage change into effect. It is probable that deviations in time are more common than those in amount.

This discussion of wage history suggests a final problem in administering the intraindustry comparison, namely, the historic differential. That is, how do arbitrators behave when an established disparity in rates conflicts with the principle of wage parity within the industry? Here the force of the intraindustry comparison is clearly paramount. In the *Pacific Gas & Electric* case, for example, the Utility Workers argued that the company's "traditional leadership" should be maintained. Kerr replied:

The doctrine of historical relationships runs directly counter to that of standardization. Standardization cannot be achieved by bringing the lower paid up to the higher

---

[49] See p. 90.

[50] In a case in which a plush mill had historically followed the wage pattern of woolens, the arbitrator continued the practice in face of the fact that product market competitors would not do so. Joan Plush Mills and Industrial Trades Union, 7 *LA* 461 (1947).

[51] Liquid Carbonic Corp. and Teamsters, 14 *LA* 655 (1950).

[52] Restaurant-Hotel Employers' Council of San Diego and Building Service Employees, 11 *LA* 469 (1948); Merchandise Warehouses of Boston and Longshoremen, 6 *LA* 521 (1946).

paid, if the higher paid insist always on being higher paid. If the lower paid were constantly to insist on standardization and the higher paid on historical differentials, the effect would be that of the dog chasing his tail. While standardization seldom occurs at one jump, it seems to be the more widely recognized and constantly effective of the two doctrines. Consequently, the argument that Pacific Gas and Electric rates should permanently be maintained a given amount above other rates is not accepted as valid.[53]

b. *Interindustry comparisons.* Though of far less significance than intraindustry comparisons, wage relationships between industries play some role in wage arbitration. That is, neutrals prefer the former when given the choice. In some instances, however, the only satisfactory comparison is between industries, such as rates for office and maintenance workers. Among all the citations of criteria in the sample, almost 14 per cent were of this type and, more important, arbitrators gave them prime weight in about 8 per cent of their awards.

"Not all wage changes," Dunlop has observed, "are equally contagious."[54] Most students of wages, in fact, are inclined to quarantine the interindustry comparison to a narrow area, and for good reason. Over time, differentials between industries shift markedly, stemming from diverse rates of basic economic change. Wage uniformity, therefore, would impose heavy burdens upon low-productivity, low-profit industries, with consequent distortions to the economy as a whole. There is a further obstruction when classification rates are contrasted, namely, the virtual impossibility of establishing comparability with respect to job content, regularity of employment, and fringe benefits between industries. As a result, arbitrators have given little consideration to the interindustry comparison generally stated (usually by unions).[55]

There are, however, limited conditions under which this standard has been given weight. It provides, for example, a rough guide to wage trends. As Pierson has pointed out, "During a period when wages are generally increasing, as in 1948, it cannot be denied that some adjustment in wages is justified in most situations in order to prevent glaring distortions in the nation's wage structure."[56] The logic of this position

[53] Pacific Gas & Electric Co. and Utility Workers, 7 *LA* 532 (1947). See also Fifth Ave. Coach Co. and Transport Workers, 4 *LA* 548 (1946); Publishers Assn. and Typographical Union, 12 *LA* 1136 (1949); California Grocers Assn. and Retail Clerks, 13 *LA* 245 (1949); Public Service Coordinated Transport and Amalgamated Street Railway Employees, 8 *LA* 530 (1947); Gary Railways and Amalgamated Street Railway Employees, 8 *LA* 641 (1947).

[54] John T. Dunlop, *Wage Determination under Trade Unions* (New York: Macmillan, 1944), p. 128.

[55] See Washington Gas Light and Suburban Gas Cos. and Chemical Workers and Office Employees, 3 *LA* 566 (1946); Fall River Textile Mfrs. Assn. and Textile Workers, 11 *LA* 984 (1949).

[56] Restaurant-Hotel Employers' Council of Southern California and Hotel and Restaurant Employees, 12 *LA* 1099 (1949).

suggests that a function of the interindustry comparison is to serve as a secondary check against those criteria to which the arbitrator gives primary weight. The 1949 Pittsburgh transit case is illustrative. The arbitrator based his ten-cent award on the historic relationship with the Chicago street railway rate. At the same time, he noted that this was the money value of the benefits granted by the dominant Pittsburgh industry, steel.[57]

A further conditioning factor, in all likelihood, is the business cycle. In the period of high activity immediately following World War II, Witte has noted, interindustry patterns were relatively influential. It was then possible for employers to pass on rising costs in higher prices. By 1948, however, a stiffening of competition in most lines led management to resist a further imposition of these patterns.[58]

Another special circumstance enhancing the importance of the interindustry comparison is a national bargaining structure. This is notably true of railroads, in which, in addition, the slow-moving dispute machinery of the Railway Labor Act creates delays that grant other industries time to set patterns. As a consequence of these factors, arbitration and emergency boards "have given almost overwhelming consideration to the criterion of comparative wage trends."[59] Differences have arisen, not over the wage standard itself, but rather over its application—base date for computation and the measurement of railway and nonrailway rates. Although it is fair to assume that interindustry comparisons are also important in wage leader cases, as might be expected, no examples appear among the arbitration awards.

A final special consideration occurs in the public utilities. It has been urged that necessary limitations on the right to strike in these industries should be balanced with an interindustry area parity policy. Hill, an industry spokesman, has argued:

> The employees of the Utility Company should not expect to enjoy wages, hours or working conditions substantially better than those enjoyed by the workers living in the area served by the Utility Company. Likewise, ... it should reasonably be expected to maintain wages, hours and working conditions that do not suffer in comparison with those enjoyed by these same workers.[60]

---

[57] Pittsburgh Railways Co. and Amalgamated Street Railway Employees, 14 *LA* 662 (1949). It is possible that arbitrators are more inclined to this view in the case of a local firm in a town with a leading industry. Similar deference was granted hosiery in the Reading transit award. Reading Street Railway Co. and Amalgamated Street Railway Employees, 6 *LA* 860 (1947).

[58] Edwin E. Witte, "Criteria in Wage Rate Determinations," *Washington University Law Quarterly* (Fall, 1949), p. 38. See also W. Rupert Maclaurin and Charles A. Myers, "Wages and the Movement of Factory Labor," in F. S. Doddy, ed., *Readings in Labor Economics* (Cambridge: Addison-Wesley, 1950), p. 124.

[59] Meyers, *op. cit.*, p. 354.

[60] Cited in Cleveland Electric Illuminating Co. and Utility Workers, 8 *LA* 600 (1947).

The reasonableness of this approach has merit, but its application presents formidable hurdles. As Taylor has observed, "It is virtually impossible to find those jobs in the community which are identical in even the important respects to the jobs found in the utilities, and making rate allowances because of differences in job content or work characteristics is scarcely an exact science."[61] Even when the parties jointly instructed the arbitrators to apply this policy, the board found it necessary to equate the interindustry comparison with intraindustry and cost-of-living factors.[62] This again suggests that in those few cases in which the interindustry comparison has validity it should be administered in terms of general wage movements rather than by contrasting classification rates.

c. *Intracompany comparisons.* Only rarely do comparisons between plants of the same firm enter wage arbitration. This is to be expected because multiunit companies often have company-wide bargaining structures, frequently apply uniform wage policies even when they have separate units, and seldom arbitrate. When such a case does reach arbitration, given comparability of operations, the full force of the intraindustry comparison is applicable, buttressed by the fact of common parentage.[63] The intracompany comparison is, in effect, a variant of the intraindustry comparison, and, therefore, is subject to the same tests and is entitled to at least equivalent weight.

d. *Intraunion comparisons.* The consideration of wage decisions based on the rates of other locals of the same labor organization poses a problem of definition. Obviously, this is a factor of great force, but it seldom arises as such. The result stems from the fact that unionism (craft and industrial) typically follows industry lines. As a result, wage comparisons between locals are normally framed in terms of the industry rather than the union.

From the standpoint of the international union, wage parity between locals in the same industry is often a vital institutional goal. To turn the coin over, interlocal rivalry over wages may disrupt the parent body. It is reported, for example, that a particular firm was able to double its rates and still earn large profits. The international union, however, opposed a large increase to avoid embarrassment with fourteen other locals in the same community.[64] In the rare case in which the problem

---

[61] Consolidated Edison System and Utility Workers, 6 LA 834 (1947).

[62] Cleveland Electric Illuminating Co. and Utility Workers, 8 *LA* 597 (1947). The notorious difficulties of administering interindustry area rates for the Bell system are treated in Emanuel Stein, "Criteria in Wage Arbitration," *New York University Law Review*, XXV (October, 1950), 727–736.

[63] Blue Print Co. and Photographic Employees, 7 *LA* 154 (1947).

[64] Social Science Research Council, Committee on Labor Market Research, "Research on Wages" (February, 1948), p. 6.

is presented in this form, therefore, the arbitrator is likely to give decisive weight to the intraunion comparison.[65]

e. *Interunion comparisons.* Wage comparisons between labor organizations arise under two conditions: (a) rival unionism—several unions in the same firm or industry competing for jurisdiction, and (b) contiguous unionism—several unions in the same firm or industry with defined jurisdictions that do not overlap. The force of the wage comparison is greater when organizations are vying with one another, since wage advantage is an instrument of institutional aggrandizement. Arbitrators, viewing the rate as a lever for recruiting members in a contest for jurisdiction, are reluctant to disturb a stabilized interunion relationship. Ross has pointed to the primacy given wage parity in those industries characterized by historic rival unionism—water transportation, longshoring, and warehousing.[66] There is merit in adding, however, that competition between unions in so intense a form occurs relatively infrequently.

A notable illustration of rival unionism is the conflict between Longshoremen and Teamsters in the San Francisco Bay warehousing industry. In 1946, the former, representing five thousand employees, settled for three and a half cents. The Teamsters, with 850 to 1,000 members, asked for sixteen cents. The arbitrator, Wyckoff, declared:

> Over the entire history of the master agreement, the adjustments negotiated by Local 860 [Teamsters] have been closely correlated with those negotiated by Local 6 [Longshoremen]. . . . The amount of the wage adjustments has been identical with . . . one exception . . .; and each of the four wage increases granted to Local 860 was preceded by the grant to Local 6, a month or so before, of an identical increase.[67]

The arbitrator awarded three and a half cents.

Great weight was attached to the historic wage relationship in the above case. In a dispute in which parity between the Molders and Stove Mounters was at issue, the arbitrator found that interunion rates over time had not been linked. As a result, he felt the imposition of the Molders' settlement "would be to deny or destroy any effective bargaining power on the part of a union situated as is Local No. 60 [Stove Mounters]."[68] A complication of rival union parity may arise when there is a substantial time lag between settlements. In 1947, for example, the Electrical Workers, the larger union, and the Pacific Gas & Electric Company agreed on 14.1 cents. The Utility Workers, though offered the same adjustment, insisted on a larger increase. The arbitrator in-

---

[65] Waterfront Warehouses and Longshoremen, 2 *LA* 136 (1946).
[66] Ross, *op. cit.*, pp. 64–68.
[67] San Francisco Employers Council and Teamsters, 7 *LA* 37 (1946).
[68] Manufacturers' Protective Assn. and Stove Mounters, 13 *LA* 905 (1949).

timated that he would have accepted the 14.1 cent formula except for developments since its negotiation—a rise in the cost of living and the emergence of an industry pattern of seventeen and a half cents. Hence he granted the latter amount.[69]

Contiguous unionism appears to have little influence upon wage determination in arbitration. In a case of this type the neutral found that the employees had nothing in common, were represented in distinct bargaining units, and had an unrelated wage history.

Because of this history, any differences herein granted cannot create an inequity. In addition, to recognize such an argument would enable the company and the union to play one organization off as against another rather than grant or deny each union whatever wage increase might be due under wage stabilization formulas.[70]

Again, emphasis upon the test of wage history is notable.

The present chapter has been concerned with the force of comparisons as applied in wage arbitration. We now turn to criteria of lesser importance in this process.

---

[69] Pacific Gas & Electric Co. and Utility Workers, 7 *LA* 528 (1947).
[70] Moe Levy & Sons and Upholsterers, 4 *LA* 782 (1946).

V. CRITERIA OF WAGE DETERMINATION: II

3. Cost of Living

THE IMPORTANCE of cost of living in wage-fixing is a function of the rate of change in the level of consumer prices. Practically speaking, this factor is of little or no significance when prices are stable, of some significance when they decline, and of considerable significance when they rise. In the year span of the sample employed here, 1945–1950, arbitrators gave prime weight to cost of living in 34 per cent of the awards. This notable statistic is to be explained, in large part, by the fact that several of these years witnessed sharp increases in the prices of goods consumers bought.

The validity of the cost-of-living argument in an inflationary peacetime period rests upon an ethical presumption, namely, that the real wages of workers should not be depreciated by price movements beyond their control. As Feis has said, "It is a simple claim. It is a claim the justice of which could be denied only under unusual circumstances."[1] The force of this contention is universally accepted by workers and unions. The great majority of employers appear to have adopted it, as well, in recent years. Almost all wage arbitrators concur.[2] Differences arise, therefore, not over the principle but over its application.

The cost-of-living criterion, like wage comparisons, is readily translatable into cents per hour. Despite variations in methods of computation and *ad hoc* disagreement over them, the calculations are within the area of the known and not that of the imponderable. Few other wage standards have this distinction. An index of consumer prices, no matter how dubious its construction, yields an exact result of percentage change which is speedily convertible into an equally exact adjustment of wage rates. The temptations of precision are difficult to resist.

Fluctuations in the cost of living are economy-wide in impact; that is, diverse sectors of the wage structure are affected in approximately equivalent degree by price movements that flow in the same direction and differ only within a narrow range. This distinguishes cost of living

---

[1] Herbert Feis, *The Settlement of Wage Disputes* (New York: Macmillan, 1921), p. 107. The Webbs have erected a Doctrine of Vested Interests, "the assumption that the wages . . . hitherto enjoyed by any section of workmen ought under no circumstances to be interfered with for the worse." Sidney and Beatrice Webb, *Industrial Democracy* (2d ed.; London: Longmans, Green, 1920), p. 562.

[2] For an exception, see Chesapeake & Potomac Telephone Co. and Maryland Fed. of Telephone Workers, 7 *LA* 630 (1947). The above line of analysis loses validity when a large segment of national product is converted to war purposes with a consequent decline in everyone's real income.

from most other standards of wage determination, which express factors within the firm (financial condition of the employer) or within the industry (intraindustry comparisons). As a result, a marked change in the price level is likely to be reflected throughout the wage structure and may appear in particular context in another form. A pattern-setting concern, for example, may increase wages because the Consumers' Price Index has risen, smaller firms following on the intra-industry comparison.

Changes in the cost of living are measured by pricing a constant "market basket" of goods and services at regular time intervals and by converting these prices into index numbers for aggregates (food, apparel, rent, etc.) as well as for all items combined. This statistical operation has been practiced for many years. Several agencies in the United States perform this function: the U. S. Bureau of Labor Statistics, the National Industrial Conference Board (a private organization under management sponsorship), and some state statistical departments for their own jurisdictions. If the disputes that reach arbitration are representative of bargaining generally, the BLS Consumers' Price Index for all practical purposes has crowded the others out of wage determination. In this discussion, therefore, it alone is taken into account.

This index is based upon a 1952 average budget of urban wage-earner and clerical-worker families. It stemmed from an exhaustive survey of expenditure patterns for these families in 1950, adjusted for price changes to 1952. The Bureau now prices three hundred items in forty-six communities of all sizes periodically. When weighted into an index, these pricings measure the average change in the cost of these goods and services to moderate income families in urban areas. An index is published monthly for the United States as a whole and for each of the twenty largest cities. The base period (100) is taken as 1947–1949.

The method of using the index in wage determination is best demonstrated by hypothetical example: The one-year contract between the ABC Mfg. Co. of Los Angeles and Local 47 of the XYZ Union expired on May 15, 1951. Failing agreement on the latter's demand for a wage increase of twenty-five cents, the parties submitted this issue to arbitration. The neutral decided to give sole weight to the Los Angeles Consumers' Price Index from the base date of the old contract, May 15, 1950. The index number at that time stood at 166.7 and rose by May 15, 1951 to 184.1, an increase of 10.4 per cent. He then applied this figure to straight-time average hourly earnings of all production workers of $1.50, yielding a general wage adjustment of 15.6 cents per hour.

In reaching this result, the arbitrator was called upon to make the following decisions: (1) to select the BLS index for Los Angeles over alternative indexes; (2) to choose the base date at the expiration of the old contract rather than some other time; (3) to use straight-time average hourly earnings in converting the price change into a wage adjustment in preference to some other measurement of wages; and (4) to apply the increase in equal amount to all employees rather than differentially.

The construction of a cost-of-living index, it has been observed, is "scarcely an exact science."[3] Before turning to the pragmatic problems of index administration in wage-fixing, there is merit in noting the more general difficulties of application as Dunlop has framed them. He raises five objections to cost of living as an "absolute" principle: (1) the index contains elements, notably food and rent, whose price movements do not necessarily coincide with changes in other wage-determining factors; (2) permanent escalation would produce a stationary real standard of life in defiance of improvements in productivity; (3) sharp differences are evident over the techniques of measurement; (4) the appropriate base date is often a source of contention; and (5) adjusting wages in response to shifts in the index may be unwise economic policy under some circumstances.[4]

It is not infrequent in arbitration for one of the parties, usually the union, to attack the index. In the *San Diego Gas & Electric* case, for example, the Electrical Workers argued that prices had risen more in San Diego than in Los Angeles, the nearest community priced by BLS; that consumption habits had changed since 1934–1936, the "market basket" pricing period of the old index, to the disadvantage of workers; and that such factors as higher income taxes and quality deterioration had not been weighed. The arbitrator was not impressed.[5] In all likelihood, this is a typical response, if for no other reason, simply because there is no numerically calculable alternative. In the case of an isolated Florida community, however, a clear unfavorable differential existed owing to higher transportation costs and utility rates; hence the arbitrator assumed an understatement by the index. Here, again, he faced the dilemma of being unable precisely to measure the difference.[6]

The principal issues in the administration of this criterion are the base period and the computation of wages. Of these, the base date is

---

[3] Z. Clark Dickinson, *Collective Wage Determination* (New York: Ronald, 1941), p. 117.

[4] John T. Dunlop, *Collective Bargaining, Principles and Cases* (Chicago: Irwin, 1949), pp. 98–100.

[5] San Diego Gas & Electric Co. and Brotherhood of Electrical Workers, 12 *LA* 245 (1949).

[6] U. S. Sugar Co. and Sugar Mill Workers, 5 *LA* 314 (1946).

more commonly raised and evokes a sharply delineated line of arbitral opinion.

The impact of alternative bases upon the range of decision-making is pointedly conveyed by the *San Diego Electric Railway* case. These possibilities offered the arbitrator a spread of forty-five cents per hour, obviously an amount far beyond the limits of acceptability. To restore real wages to the level of each of the base periods, he would have been required to grant the following adjustments:[7]

```
1935–1939  . . . . . . . . . . . . . . . . . . . . . . . . . . . . .$–.24
January 1941
    (Base date for Little Steel formula). . . . . . . .  –.10
V-J Day . . . . . . . . . . . . . . . . . . . . . . . . . . . . . . .   .00
June 1946
    (Effective date of next to last contract). . . .  +.21
June 1947
    (Effective date of last contract)  . . . . . . . . . . .  +.11
```

Base period manipulation, as this illustration shows, presents grave hazards. Arbitrators have guarded themselves against these risks by working out a quite generally accepted rule: the base for computing cost-of-living adjustments shall be the effective date of the last contract (that is, the expiration date of the second last agreement).[8] The justification here is identical with that taken by arbitrators in the case of a reopening clause, namely, the presumption that the most recent negotiations disposed of all the factors of wage determination. "To go behind such a date," a transit board has noted, "would of necessity require a re-litigation of every preceding arbitration between the parties and a re-examination of every preceding bargain concluded between them."[9] This assumption appears to be made even in the absence of evidence that the parties explicitly disposed of cost of living in their negotiations. Where the legislative history demonstrates that this issue was considered, the holding becomes so much the stronger.

This line of reasoning rests upon the past rather than the prospective behavior of the index, the former being the more common method

---

[7] San Diego Electric Railway Co. and Amalgamated Street Railway Employees, 11 *LA* 460 (1948).

[8] San Diego Electric Railway Co. and Amalgamated Street Railway Employees, 11 *LA* 458 (1948); Los Angeles Transit Lines and Amalgamated Street Railway Employees, 11 *LA* 118 (1948); Bay Cities Transit Co. and Amalgamated Street Railway Employees, 11 *LA* 747 (1948); Public Service Coordinated Transport and Amalgamated Street Railway Employees, 11 *LA* 1037 (1948); San Diego Gas & Electric Co. and Brotherhood of Electrical Workers, 12 *LA* 245 (1949).

[9] Public Service Coordinated Transport and Amalgamated Street Railway Employees, 11 *LA* 1050 (1948).

of calculating a cost-of-living wage change. Where, as occasionally happens, the parties in their last negotiations discounted a future price movement, the expiration date of the prior contract is not appropriate. In this contingency, presumably, the arbitrator would have to make an adjustment for the difference between the estimated and actual performance of the index.[10]

The *New York Times* case is a unique illustration of an award based upon the anticipated rather than the prior performance of the index. Dunlop ventured into this treacherous area with hesitation since, as he pointed out, "no arbitrator has a reliable crystal ball and . . . public policy statements by responsible government officials have cautioned against such anticipations." He was, apparently, persuaded to do so because he had awarded a firm two-year contract and because the recent outbreak of the Korean War created the reasonable presumption that prices would rise.[11] In such a case, of course, the cost-of-living criterion is no longer precisely translatable into cents per hour, inasmuch as one of the factors in the computation, the price change, is now an inexact estimate.

In computing a cost-of-living change the possibility of manipulating the price lever is matched on the wage side. This is particularly the case under an incentive system or when substantial overtime is worked. The usual practice to minimize these difficulties is to employ straight-time average hourly earnings or base rates in computing shifts in the wage level. This is on the assumption that a cost-of-living adjustment should go even-handedly to all employees without regard to the rewards of individual effort or long hours.

In the process of balancing conflicting standards of wage determination, arbitrators tend to give heavy weight to cost of living over others. That is, they incline to the view that the employer is obliged to maintain real wages in the face of rising prices except under extraordinary conditions. As Pierson has pointed out:

> While the Arbitrator cannot agree with the view that wage rates in every industry must keep pace with increases in the cost of living, regardless of profit levels and every other consideration, the fact remains that only under the most unusual circumstances is an industry justified in not meeting this minimum standard of performance.[12]

---

[10] George W. Taylor, "Criteria in the Wage Bargain," *Proceedings of New York University First Annual Conference on Labor* (Albany: Bender, 1948), pp. 77–78; Twin City Rapid Transit Co. and Amalgamated Street Railway Employees, 10 *LA* 581 (1948).

[11] *New York Times* and Newspaper Guild, 15 *LA* 333 (1950).

[12] Restaurant-Hotel Employers' Council of Southern California and Hotel and Restaurant Employees, 12 *LA* 1099 (1949). See also Merchandise Warehouses of Boston and Longshoremen, 6 *LA* 521 (1946); Moeller Instrument Co. and United Electrical

In a case in which the employer clearly established extreme financial hardship, however, the arbitrator moderated the amount the employees deserved under the index. He wrote: "Economic factors of such magnitude [reductions of 40 per cent in sales and 30 per cent in prices] cannot be ignored in the setting of wage rates."[13]

The preceding discussion of arbitral conduct has assumed a rising price level. The quite precise escalator arrangement between the Consumers' Price Index and arbitrators' awards, however, moves in only one direction: up. The economic and institutional forces that lead unions vigorously to resist wage cuts have been noted.[14] Third parties, in turn, reflect those pressures. In addition, as Feis has observed, the ethical content is drained from the cost-of-living criterion when prices decline. Employers seldom argue that "justice or social welfare require that wages must be reduced just because the cost of living falls. The ethical presumption inclines the other way." As a consequence, arbitrators are likely to cut wages because the employer has fallen on hard times. If, at the same time, consumer prices have dropped, reductions "meet with less resistance than they would otherwise." The cause, in other words, lies in the employer rather than in the index.[15]

Given this line of arbitral reasoning, it follows that conflicting standards win more weight when the cost of living drops than when it rises. An employer's suggestion that he should take account of a modest decline in the index led Dash to observe that linking wages solely to cost of living would "deny the importance of specific factors in a given industry that might indicate very sound reasons for wage adjustments to vary from the general trend in the cost-of-living."[16]

4. *Financial Condition of the Employer*

This unorthodox and rather heavy-handed title constitutes an attempt to devise a meaningful phrase to describe what the parties and arbitrators actually deal with in wage cases. The conventional slogan—ability to pay—is deficient on several counts. For one, the employer's

---

Workers, 6 *LA* 639 (1947); Pacific Gas & Electric Co. and Utility Workers, 7 *LA* 528 (1947); Associated General Contractors and Operating Engineers, 9 *LA* 201 (1947); Restaurant-Hotel Employers' Council of San Diego and Building Service Employees, 11 *LA* 469 (1948).

[13] National Bedding & Upholstery Mfrs. Board of Trade and Furniture Workers, 10 *LA* 814 (1948).

[14] See p. 8, above.

[15] Herbert Feis, *Principles of Wage Settlement* (New York: Wilson, 1924), pp. 247–248, 250.

[16] Pittsburgh Railways Co. and Amalgamated Street Railway Employees, 14 *LA* 669 (1949). See also Puget Sound Navigation Co. and Masters, Mates and Pilots, 13 *LA* 255 (1949).

typical plea is negative, *in*ability to pay. For the purpose of precision in this discussion this concept is confined to the comparatively rare contention that a wage increase or failure to cut rates would imperil the marginal firm. A second inadequacy of "ability to pay" is that the usual argument is less extreme than this language suggests on its face. Normally the employer contends that a prospective wage action would be a secondary financial embarrassment. He may note, for example, that stiffening price competition necessitates cost retrenchment without suggesting that failure to cut wages will knock the firm out of business. The term "financial condition of the employer," then, shall include these three relatively distinct notions: affirmative ability to pay as justification for an increase, inability to pay in face of a threat to survival, and, most commonly, moderation in wage policy reflecting less than satisfactory business conditions.

Assuming this comprehensive definition, the financial-condition-of-the-employer criterion is commonly invoked in wage arbitration, constituting 14 per cent of the total number of citations in the sample. The differences between groups are very sharp. Almost a third of employer arguments are of this type as contrasted with fewer than 3 per cent on the union side. Arbitrators give it some weight in nearly 12 per cent of their decisions but make it the primary or sole factor in only 3.5 per cent. Dunlop, furthermore, goes so far as to observe that "ability to pay" is an explicit or implied consideration in virtually every wage decision. The presumption of the union's demand is that the employer can stand it and of his offer that he cannot.[17] It is hardly necessary to explore the semantic issues inherent in this position to draw the simple conclusion that financial condition of the employer is a key standard of wage determination.

The financial-condition criterion provokes sharp conflicts between the opposite sides of the bargaining table as well as diversity of viewpoint on each side. The effort here to sift out the policies of unions and employers, therefore, is subject to mutation in a particular context.

Speaking very broadly, the employer's financial position is a fundamental determinant of his wage policy. This is readily seen at the extremes. If he is operating at a very high profit level and anticipates its continuance, there is the likelihood that his wage program will be liberal. If, on the other hand, he is losing money and foresees no improvement, he will shut his plant and offer no wages at all. This factor, doubtless, conditions management policy in the intermediate zone as well. Profit position, then, influences the direction of the employer's offer, although it seldom determines the precise amount. As one man-

---

[17] Dunlop, *op. cit.*, pp. 100–101.

agement representative has observed, "The earnings position of the company is not directly considered, but it certainly has a strong effect on our frame of mind."[18] In arbitration, of course, only the negative side of this criterion appears. That is, if the employer agrees with the union that he can afford to pay the increase demanded, there will be no dispute to submit to arbitration.

Union policies, generally speaking, vary for each of the three aspects of the definition of this criterion set forth above. When the employer is making a great deal of money, his employees expect to share in his prosperity. Union wage policy, naturally, reflects this viewpoint.[19] The General Motors strike after V-J Day notably illustrated this in the Auto Workers' insistence upon having a look at the corporation's books. Difficulties of conversion, however, reduce to zero the number of cases in which an upward adjustment is escalated with profits. The employer's favorable position, rather, serves as a supporting member for another and more direct wage standard.

In the case of the marginal firm teetering at the brink of extinction pressures on the union are in the direction of giving great weight to the employer's finances. That is, when the alternative to a wage cut (or no increase) is loss of the employees' jobs, the labor organization can scarcely fail to elect employment. There are two reasons: workers prefer jobs over higher rates and unions prefer more over fewer members. As Taylor has put it, "Unions couldn't live with a wage policy that puts too many people out of work."[20] This labor attitude is more common in a highly competitive and partly unionized industry, like hosiery, in which the unorganized sector enjoys a favorable wage differential. The case of the monopoly public utility is not so neat, since the bankrupt as well as the profitable firm must continue to operate and so to offer jobs. As Zimring, representing the Street Railway Employees, has argued:

> The employees of a public utility should not subsidize their employers by working for sub-standard wages. . . . If the public wishes to have an efficient transit system it should pay for it the same way it pays for other public needs. This may be done by having private companies with fare structures sufficient to pay expenses including fair and adequate wages; or it may be done by having a public agency furnish transportation and finance it in the same manner as other publicly owned utilities, i.e. through payment by the users, freedom from certain taxes and, when necessary,

---

[18] Quoted in W. S. Woytinsky and Associates, *Labor and Management Look at Collective Bargaining* (New York: Twentieth Century Fund, 1949), p. 89.

[19] Edwin E. Witte, "Criteria in Wage Rate Determinations," *Washington University Law Quarterly* (Fall, 1949), p. 34.

[20] Taylor, *op. cit.*, p. 73. See also Trailways of New England and Amalgamated Street Railway Employees, 7 *LA* 319 (1947) and Beach Transit Corp. and Transport Workers, 11 *LA* 639 (1948).

through subsidies. . . . Boards of arbitration should not be asked to take sides in the question of private or public ownership and to refuse an otherwise justified wage increase on the ground that it might bring about public ownership.[21]

In the most common situation—the employer must retrench but there is little likelihood that he will shut down—unions are disinclined to give him the benefit of the doubt. As a business agent has put it: "If an employer is not able to pay, he should find ways of running his business more efficiently—but he should not take it out of the hides of his employees."[22] This view stems, in part, from the knowledge that the wage factor is only one among several entering into cost. Unions prefer that others make the first sacrifice. Also, there is no assurance that acceptance of a wage cut will actually put the employer back on his feet. Finally, unions, and especially workers, tend to be suspicious of gloomy financial reports and of their authors, the accountants. For these reasons labor organizations normally urge that financial adversity be ignored. "There is little evidence," Reynolds notes, "that union leaders think in terms of a demand curve for labor, or that they try to estimate the effect of different wage levels on the volume of employment in the industry."[23]

In the face of these management and labor attitudes toward the financial-capacity criterion, arbitrators have three alternatives: first, to give it decisive weight; second, to ignore it; and, finally, to accord it some but not controlling influence. The problem almost invariably arises in negative form: the employer argues that he cannot pay the proposed increase (or must have a wage cut) and the union counters that his plea should be disregarded. Hence the three options revolve about the matter so framed.

The great majority of arbitrators refuse to grant the employer's impaired financial standing decisive weight. In fact, only one case was found in which the neutral regarded it as controlling. In the *Auburn Shoe Manufacturers* award, Charles H. Cole turned down a wage increase supported by a rise in the cost of living because:

> An arbitrator must always keep in mind . . . the fact that in an industry as competitive as this one a decision economically unjustifiable may indeed be a dubious victory for a union. Therefore, we must examine the condition of the industry. . . . The shoe market has entered into a period of less than full employment. Lay-offs, short-weeks, and cuts in production are prevalent in many of the leading shoe centers. Moreover, it appears that there are growing manufacturing areas in which labor costs are so much lower than in this area that it is evident that a period of reduced

---

[21] Capital Transit Co. and Amalgamated Street Railway Employees, 9 *LA* 701 (1947).
[22] Cited in Woytinsky, *op. cit.*, p. 80.
[23] Lloyd G. Reynolds, *Labor Economics and Labor Relations* (New York: Prentice-Hall, 1949), p. 382.

demand for shoes would have serious consequences upon the employment level in this community.[24]

The much more common ruling is that the financial standard is not controlling. "I can see no justification," Wasservogel has held, "for the view that ability to pay is an absolute determinant in wage fixing."[25] Miller spelled out the reasoning for this position in the *Waterfront Employers* award. The industry urged denial of a wage increase in order to facilitate the revival of intercoastal shipping as against railway and trucking competition. The arbitrator replied:

> The employers have no better claim to whatever relief toward the revival of this part of their business would result from the denial here, of a cost of living wage adjustment than the longshoremen would have to seek a further improvement in their wage standards upon the basis of the size of the employers' past profits or the amounts of their assets. There is nothing in the record to show that in the past the wage rates of the longshoremen have been directly related to profit or loss contingencies. The employers and the longshoremen have never been partners or joint venturers in the employers' business. When the employers have made profits the longshoremen were not offered a share of them nor could they have rightly demanded to participate. . . . The precise question here is whether the problems of management, connected with the revival of domestic trade in Pacific Coast shipping, offer a compelling reason for outright denial of the Union's claim to an interim wage adjustment based upon increased living costs. For the reasons stated, the answer is that they do not.[26]

The second alternative, entirely ignoring this criterion, receives a similar response from arbitrators. The great majority are unwilling to take this extreme position; a small minority dissent. The latter viewpoint was adopted by Wyckoff in the *California Street Cable Railway* case. The union argued that the cable car operators should be paid the scale of the much more numerous employees of the San Francisco municipal system. The company contended that any increase would cause it to shut down, and the arbitrator accepted this claim. He, nevertheless, ruled that "these wages should be fixed without regard to the financial condition of the company or its ability to continue in business."[27] Most

[24] Auburn Shoe Mfrs. Assn. and Lewiston-Auburn Shoe Workers, 11 *LA* 597 (1948).

[25] Fifth Ave. Coach Co. and Transport Workers, 4 *LA* 575 (1946). See also Camburn and United Electrical Workers, 6 *LA* 636 (1947); Birmingham Electric Co. and Amalgamated Street Railway Employees, 7 *LA* 673 (1947); Painting and Decorating Employers of San Diego and Painters, 7 *LA* 769 (1947); St. Louis Public Service Co. and Amalgamated Street Railway Employees, 8 *LA* 397 (1947); Triboro Coach Corp. and Amalgamated Street Railway Employees, 8 *LA* 478 (1947); Puget Sound Navigation Co. and Inlandboatmen, 8 *LA* 563 (1947); Indianapolis Railways and Amalgamated Street Railway Employees, 9 *LA* 319 (1947).

[26] Waterfront Employers Assn. and Longshoremen and Warehousemen, 9 *LA* 179 (1947).

[27] California Street Cable Railway Co. and Amalgamated Street Railway Employees, 7 *LA* 95 (1947). For a restatement of this position by the same arbitrator, see Pacific

arbitrators, however, refuse to disregard financial hardship. As Myers
has put it, "I cannot agree with the Union that the question of ability
to pay is of no concern. It should hardly be necessary to point out that
continuity of employment in this plant depends upon the ability of
the employer to meet payrolls and other expenses from revenues."[28]

As the discussion of polar positions suggests, most arbitrators are
found in the temperate zone. For them, financial hardship is one among
several criteria, deserving of a fluctuating weight in response to the
facts of a particular wage dispute. They approach this standard with
some hesitancy, stemming from their relative unfamiliarity with profits
as contrasted with wages and from the difficulties of translating the
firm's position precisely into a wage determination. Inasmuch as the
middle ground permits of no easy rule to dispose of the employer's plea,
the arbitrator must examine each situation exhaustively and upon its
own merits. Facts, naturally, vary from case to case, with the consequence that there are few real generalizations.

One conclusion arbitrators often reach is that other standards should
generate the basic direction of the wage movement but that demonstrable financial hardship should limit the distance that it travels. As
Singer has put it, "On the facts . . . I find that inability to pay . . . may
not be used as a bar to the granting of a wage increase, but rather as a
limitation on the amount to be granted."[29] A rather neat illustration

---

American Shipowners Assn. and Communications Assn., 9 *LA* 912 (1948). See also
Puget Sound Navigation Co. and Marine Engineers, 11 *LA* 1100 (1948).

[28] Art Chrome Co. and Furniture Workers, 11 *LA* 935–936 (1948). See also River
Valley Tissue Mills and Paper Workers, 3 *LA* 245 (1946); Merchandise Warehouses of
Boston and Longshoremen, 6 *LA* 521 (1946); Sosna Brothers and Optical Workers,
6 *LA* 846 (1947); Champion Aero Metal Products and United Electrical Workers, 7
LA 278 (1947); Trailways of New England and Amalgamated Street Railway Em-
ployees, 7 *LA* 319 (1947); Painting and Decorating Employers of San Diego and
Painters, 7 *LA* 769 (1947); Kansas City Public Service Co. and Amalgamated Street
Railway Employees, 8 *LA* 149 (1947); St. Louis Public Service Co. and Amalgamated
Street Railway Employees, 8 *LA* 397 (1947); Roberts Pressure Valve Co. and Architects,
Engineers, Chemists and Technicians, 8 *LA* 665 (1947); Georgia Power Co. and
Amalgamated Street Railway Employees, 8 *LA* 691 (1947); Indianapolis Railways and
Amalgamated Street Railway Employees, 9 *LA* 319 (1947); Atlantic City Transporta-
tion Co. and Amalgamated Street Railway Employees, 9 *LA* 577 (1948); Capital
Transit Co. and Amalgamated Street Railway Employees, 9 *LA* 666 (1947); Twin
City Rapid Transit Co. and Amalgamated Street Railway Employees, 10 *LA* 581
(1948); National Bedding & Upholstery Mfrs. Board of Trade and Furniture Workers,
10 *LA* 813 (1948); Los Angeles Transit Lines and Amalgamated Street Railway Employees, 11 *LA* 118 (1948); Auburn Shoe Mfrs. Assn. and Lewiston-Auburn Shoe
Workers, 11 *LA* 594 (1948); Beach Transit Corp. and Transport Workers, 11 *LA* 639
(1948); Greater Newark Hotel Assn. and Hotel and Restaurant Employees, 13 *LA*
384 (1949); Full-Fashioned Hosiery Mfrs. and Hosiery Workers, 14 *LA* 321 (1950).

[29] Roberts Pressure Valve Co. and Architects, Engineers, Chemists and Technicians,
8 *LA* 668 (1947).

is the *Bay Cities Transit* award. Cost of living justified an increase of eleven or thirteen cents (depending upon the base date selected); prevailing rates in transit might have supported eight or nine cents; and the pattern in industry generally clustered at ten to thirteen cents. A balancing of these factors would have yielded ten or eleven cents. Nevertheless, the arbitration board, in deference to the firm's financial circumstances, moderated the award to an average of six cents, to be given in two steps of four cents for the first and eight cents for the second half-year of the contract term.[30]

Further generalization becomes more difficult because of divergencies in arbitral viewpoints. Since most arbitrators accept the principle that a wage determination requires a balancing of criteria, the basic question becomes: how much weight does financial hardship deserve when measured by other wage standards? In the cases, the other criteria consist almost exclusively of the intraindustry comparison and the cost of living.

Most arbitrators incline to give more influence to the intraindustry comparison than to financial hardship, provided that both are of roughly equivalent validity. That is, a tight comparison tends to carry greater weight than a clear showing of distress. If one is not substantiated, of course, the other gains relatively in force. An illustration of the general rule is the *Triboro Coach* case. The company demonstrated that it operated at a deficit and the union showed that wages were low for transit in the city. "The inability of the company to pay," the board held, "should not prevent the employees from receiving fair compensation for their work. It cannot be a justification for fixing its employees' wages below the lowest wages presently paid for comparable services by comparable employers within this area."[31] This position is not uni-

[30] Bay Cities Transit Co. and Amalgamated Street Railway Employees, 11 *LA* 747 (1948). This case was unusual in that the submission agreement required the board to give heavy weight to the financial factor. See also River Valley Tissue Mills and Paper Workers, 3 *LA* 245 (1946); Scranton Metal Casket Works and Local Industrial Union, 3 *LA* 370 (1946); Merchandise Warehouses of Boston and Longshoremen, 6 *LA* 521 (1946); Moeller Instrument Co. and United Electrical Workers, 6 *LA* 639 (1947); Sosna Brothers and Optical Workers, 6 *LA* 846 (1947); Champion Aero Metal Products and United Electrical Workers, 7 *LA* 278 (1947); Capital Transit Co. and Amalgamated Street Railway Employees, 9 *LA* 666 (1947); National Bedding & Upholstery Mfrs. and Furniture Workers, 10 *LA* 813 (1948); Los Angeles Transit Lines and Amalgamated Street Railway Employees, 11 *LA* 118 (1948); Art Chrome Co. and Furniture Workers, 11 *LA* 932 (1948); Dairyland Power Coop. and Brotherhood of Electrical Workers, 14 *LA* 737 (1950).

[31] Triboro Coach Corp. and Amalgamated Street Railway Employees, 8 *LA* 480 (1947). See also International Braid Co. and Textile Workers, 6 *LA* 911 (1947); California Street Cable Railway Co. and Amalgamated Street Railway Employees, 7 *LA* 91 (1947); Painting & Decorating Employers of San Diego and Painters, 7 *LA* 769 (1947); Kansas City Public Service Co. and Amalgamated Street Railway Employees, 8

versally held; a few arbitrators give greater weight to the hardship plea. In the *Sosna Brothers* case, for example, Rosenfarb found the wages "subaverage" for the industry in the area. He argued, nevertheless, that this consideration "must be modified in accordance with the employer's ability to pay."[32] Sometimes the conflicting criteria are unequally substantiated with greater weight accruing to the one with firmer support. In the *Boston Warehouses* case, for example, the arbitrator was more impressed with the industry's dismal competitive position than he was with the union's desire to establish wage parity with other groups. This was because he could find no historic uniformity in either the timing or amount of wage movements between Boston warehousemen, on the one hand, and Boston longshoremen or New York warehousemen, on the other.[33]

Arbitrators have evolved no clear line on the weight to be assigned financial hardship in relation to cost of living. The only generalization that is perfectly safe is that they do not feel that a wage claim based on rising living costs should be dismissed out of hand because the employer is distressed.

The awards reflect two conflicting views: first, that the cost-of-living factor is paramount, and, second, that it deserves some weight but must be moderated by the hardship consideration. The former has been expressed by France: "The workers' immediate need for pay relief is extreme. The stockholders' rights to profits must, in our system, follow upon and not precede the ability of the workers to live."[34] Rosenfarb has voiced the more moderate position:

> In an era of rising cost of living, an increase in wages must be considered as much a part of the business equation as rising costs in raw materials. . . . Nevertheless, an unfavorable business picture of the individual employer . . . must serve as a limitation on labor's ability to improve its conditions.[35]

LA 149 (1947); St. Louis Public Service Co. and Amalgamated Street Railway Employees, 8 *LA* 397 (1947); Atlantic City Transportation Co. and Amalgamated Street Railway Employees, 9 *LA* 577 (1948); Capital Transit Co. and Amalgamated Street Railway Employees, 9 *LA* 666 (1947); Twin City Rapid Transit Co. and Amalgamated Street Railway Employees, 10 *LA* 581 (1948); Dairyland Power Coop. and Brotherhood of Electrical Workers, 14 *LA* 737 (1950).

[32] Sosna Brothers and Optical Workers, 6 *LA* 849 (1947). See also Moeller Instrument Co. and United Electrical Workers, 6 *LA* 639 (1947).

[33] Merchandise Warehouses of Boston and Longshoremen, 6 *LA* 521 (1946). See also Champion Aero Metal Products and United Electrical Workers, 7 *LA* 278 (1947).

[34] U. S. Sugar Co. and Sugar Mill Workers, 5 *LA* 320 (1946). See also Merchandise Warehouses of Boston and Longshoremen, 6 *LA* 521 (1946); Moeller Instrument Co. and United Electrical Workers, 6 *LA* 639 (1947); Waterfront Employers Assn. and Longshoremen and Warehousemen, 9 *LA* 172 (1947); Twin City Rapid Transit Co. and Amalgamated Street Railway Employees, 10 *LA* 581 (1948).

[35] Sosna Brothers and Optical Workers, 6 *LA* 849 (1947). See also Champion Aero Metal Products and United Electrical Workers, 7 *LA* 278 (1947); Roberts Pressure

The two criteria heretofore discussed, intraindustry comparisons and cost of living, normally arise in wage arbitrations of secondary importance. It is likely that arbitrators would lend greater weight to financial hardship in relation to these standards in so-called "key bargains." As David Cole pointed out in the *Atlantic City Transportation* case, "If this Company were asked to pioneer in establishing high or unusual wages . . . this [financial distress] would be a strong deterrent."[36] Pattern-setting wage disputes, as has already been noted, virtually never reach arbitration.

An aspect of the financial-condition criterion which sometimes arises is whether a wage increase should be made contingent upon a related adjustment in the price of the product or service sold. This problem frequently comes up in transit and rarely in other industries. Street railway companies often argue that a wage increase should be denied because their fares can be raised only with the approval of a public utilities commission. "The Company feels trapped between the ceiling on its fare structure prescribed by a regulatory commission and the economic demands of the Union."[37] The labor organization in this industry counters that wages should be set with exclusive regard to wage-determining criteria and that any resultant increase in costs should then be presented to the public utility body as a basis for a fare adjustment.

Arbitrators reveal no conflict in viewpoint in devising a rule covering this point: they unanimously refuse to give weight to the price factor or to grant contingent wage adjustments. In so concluding, arbitrators have followed the precedent in the railroad industry, in which the parties or emergency boards fix wages without regard to tariffs, leaving the carriers to submit independent pleas to the Interstate Commerce Commission for higher fare structures. McCoy has presented the reasoning for separating the functions.

The [Gary Railways] Company's argument really amounts to a contention that this Board of Arbitration should fix wage rates that will assure a fair return to the Company on investment, upon the assumption that a Public Service Commission and the courts will fail in their duty. I can make no such assumption. And even if I could and did, I would not feel that it was my duty to compel employees to subsidize the Company. . . . Suppose that General Motors had made a contract for the sale to the Company of a number of buses, by a contract so ambiguously worded as to price that

Valve Co. and Architects, Engineers, Chemists and Technicians, 8 *LA* 665 (1947); Capital Transit Co. and Amalgamated Street Railway Employees, 9 *LA* 666 (1947); National Bedding & Upholstery Mfrs. and Furniture Workers, 10 *LA* 813 (1948); Bay Cities Transit Co. and Amalgamated Street Railway Employees, 11 *LA* 747 (1948).

[36] Atlantic City Transportation Co. and Amalgamated Street Railway Employees, 9 *LA* 580 (1948).

[37] Twin City Rapid Transit Co. and Amalgamated Street Railway Employees, 10 *LA* 588 (1948).

the parties resorted to arbitration to fix a fair price. At the hearing General Motors introduces evidence as to cost and as to general practice with respect to fair profits, tending to prove that the price should be fixed at $30,000 a bus; the Gary Railways replies with evidence that if it has to pay that price it would have to get rate relief, and perhaps could not. Would any board of arbitration award a price of $15,000 per bus based on such an argument? Wage rates are fixed by objective standards, just as are the prices of materials and products. It is the duty of this Board to fix wage rates on the basis of those objective standards. Public Service Commission and courts must determine for themselves what their duties are.[38]

The discussion thus far has assumed a negative frame for the financial criterion, that the employer requires cost relief in the face of hardship. Occasionally, this standard is turned about, the union arguing that an increase should be granted because the firm is affirmatively able to stand it. Only two awards of this sort were found, and in both the arbitrator refused to be swayed by the argument. In the *World-Telegram* case the newspaper's salary rates were found to meet prevailing metropolitan standards. "The suggestion," David Cole held, "that it is financially able to pay more and therefore should, is, in the absence of other circumstances calling for wage increases, not persuasive."[39] This conclusion was reaffirmed within the special framework of the public utility in the *Pacific Gas & Electric* award. The arbitrator pointed out that within practical limits the monopoly utility always had capacity to pay because the public would buy its services at any price. Hence it would be unfair to consumers to base wages upon affirmative ability to grant an increase.[40]

The happy air of certainty that pervades the measurement of wage changes based upon comparisons and cost of living evaporates in face of the financial-condition criterion. This factor is bedeviled with imprecision and arbitrators have not been noticeably more successful than the parties in working out solutions. There are two basic issues:

    1. What standards are to be used in determining the employer's financial situation?

---

[38] Gary Railways and Amalgamated Street Railway Employees, 8 *LA* 645 (1947). See also Reading Street Railway Co. and Amalgamated Street Railway Employees, 6 *LA* 860 (1947); Georgia Power Co. and Amalgamated Street Railway Employees, 8 *LA* 691 (1947); Indianapolis Railways and Amalgamated Street Railway Employees, 9 *LA* 319 (1947); Atlantic City Transportation Co. and Amalgamated Street Railway Employees, 9 *LA* 577 (1948); Capital Transit Co. and Amalgamated Street Railway Employees, 9 *LA* 666 (1947); Twin City Rapid Transit Co. and Amalgamated Street Railway Employees, 10 *LA* 581 (1948); National Zinc Co. and Acid and Smelter Workers, 11 *LA* 585 (1948); Puget Sound Navigation Co. and Masters, Mates and Pilots, 13 *LA* 255 (1949); Pittsburgh Railways Co. and Amalgamated Street Railway Employees, 14 *LA* 662 (1949).
[39] *New York World-Telegram* and Newspaper Guild, 12 *LA* 948 (1949).
[40] Pacific Gas & Electric Co. and Utility Workers, 7 *LA* 528 (1947).

2. Assuming a finding of hardship, how is it to be translated into a wage decision?

With respect to the first problem, employers have sought to establish financial hardship by citing a wide variety of factors. Kuhn reports that in transit "inability to pay has been defined . . . in about as many ways as there have been firms in arbitration."[41] Some were these: a recession from peak earnings; a potential impairment of the company's credit standing; reverses in some aspect of operations (i.e., vehicle miles per hour, ratio of labor costs to receipts, rising material costs); a rate of return lower than the legal limit; the need to induce new capital or to abandon improvements already planned; and a failure to meet interest payments. The fact that such a disparate body of evidence is advanced suggests that no part of it is decisive.

From the standpoint of the arbitrator, the establishment of hardship may be reduced to a small group of subquestions. The first is whether the employer is fully coöperative in revealing his situation. This is more a matter of procedure than of finance. As a result, it has been possible for neutrals to work out a fairly consistent line of decisions. They tend to rule that the burden of proof rests wholly upon the employer and that he must make a full disclosure ("opening the books"). In the absence of a willingness to assume both these obligations, arbitrators are disinclined to give weight to a plea of financial hardship.[42] In effect, this rule is a device to avoid the substantive difficulties. Oftentimes, however, this easy out is not available to the arbitrator.

The second and far more difficult subquestion is, what standards should apply in determining a reasonable profit? This issue must be faced, because the presumption underlying the employer's plea of hardship is that his return is inadequate. The unhappy arbitrator is then caught between the compulsion to meet the issue and the absence of criteria for disposing of it. The record in fixing a "fair profit" in public utility regulation, in excess profits taxation, and in contract renegotiation is less than reassuring. To cite only one among many thorny matters that arise: should the arbitrator consider profits before or after taxes? Even if objective standards for determining reasonableness ex-

---

[41] Alfred Kuhn, *Arbitration in Transit, and Evaluation of Wage Criteria*, Labor Relations Series (Philadelphia: University of Pennsylvania Press, 1952), p. 78.

[42] North Jersey Broadcasting Co. and Brotherhood of Electrical Workers, 3 *LA* 437 (1946); Master Barbers and Barbers and Beauty Culturists, 5 *LA* 269 (1946); J. F. D. Mfg. Co. and United Electrical Workers, 7 *LA* 241 (1947); A. S. Beck Shoe Corp. and Longshoremen and Warehousemen, 7 *LA* 924 (1947); Brockton Gas Light Co. and Utility Workers, 8 *LA* 124 (1947); Mye Drug Co. and Retail, Wholesale and Department Store Union, 9 *LA* 146 (1947); Puget Sound Navigation Co. and Marine Engineers, 11 *LA* 1100 (1948); Mason Contractors' Assn. of Detroit and Bricklayers, 12 *LA* 909 (1949).

isted, the labor arbitrator is usually uncomfortable in the profit area. This is because he is rarely competent in accounting and because employers are seldom willing to submit that issue in full in wage arbitration. The analysis in this paragraph hardly constitutes an answer to the question with which it began.

A third subquestion is, what is the appropriate time interval? Should the arbitrator look to the past or to the future? Again, there is no reliable rule. This is evident in the fact that unions and employers manipulate the time lever opportunistically. When arbitration occurs as a depression sets in, for example, the union is likely to point to the prior year and the employer to the prospective one.[43] Although it hardly establishes a rule, the *Fall River Textile* award constitutes an isolated example of a case in which the arbitrator cast his vote for the future and in doing so raised a key problem that plagued his choice. The northern cotton textile industry had enjoyed prosperity until shortly before the arbitration when business conditions turned for the worse. As a result, the union pointed to the level of profits in the prior period and the employers to that in the anticipated period. Brown wrote:

> The decision . . . must rest, not upon knowledge or certainty, but upon judgments which are all too susceptible to error. Still further difficulties are introduced by the fact that many of the judgments, and probably the most important ones, involve not *what is,* or *what has happened,* but *what is likely to happen.* . . .
>
> Any precise prediction of what will happen in the ensuing few months lies, of course, in the realm of prophecy. The arbitrator holds no union card in that particular guild. But, to the best of his ability, he must make judgment with respect to the probable future course of events.[44]

He foresaw a dim outlook for the industry, and, accordingly, denied the union's demand for a wage increase.

In summary, there are no satisfactory criteria for precisely determining the employer's financial situation in relation to a wage dispute. Where possible to do so, arbitrators have avoided the issue by placing the burden of proof upon the employer. When compelled to measure the firm's financial standing, they have failed to evolve general rules. In other words, they have related the issue to the particular bargaining relationship and have reached decisions based only in part on the balance sheet.

The second basic issue, the translation of a finding of hardship into a cents-per-hour wage adjustment, is no more yielding of solution. That

---

[43] George Soule, *Wage Arbitration, Selected Cases, 1920–1924* (New York: Macmillan, 1928), pp. 25–26.

[44] Fall River Textile Mfrs. Assn. and Textile Workers, 11 *LA* 988, 990–991 (1949).

is, bad business conditions may compel a reduction, but there is no yardstick to calculate the amount. Is there five cents or ten cents worth of "badness"?

Ross has demonstrated that "in the chain between wage rates and employment . . . there is a great deal of free play; and, as a result, the initial and final links are so loosely connected that for practical purposes they must be regarded as largely independent."[45] The contrary argument assumes four interconnected steps: (1) that the level of wages is related to the labor cost of production; (2) that labor cost is an important factor in total cost; (3) that total cost affects the price of the product; and (4) that price affects sales and so the volume of production and employment. At the first step, Ross notes, there is little assurance that a wage cut will actually reduce labor cost. This is because labor cost is determined by both wages and productivity; the latter fluctuates quite independently of the former and is seldom predictable. The second step falters on the fact that of the three cost factors—labor, materials, and overhead—labor is least important in most industries since it is normally a relatively small part of total cost. Further, these factors often move in opposite directions simultaneously, for example, a decline in wages and a rise in overhead, so that manipulation of the former may accompany the opposite result in total cost. Third, price decisions are often made for reasons which have nothing to do with cost. Finally, prices have only a loose relationship to sales and employment. Many industries operate with administered prices; with nonrigid prices the sales advantage to the firm of a price cut may be wiped out by similar reductions by competitors.[46]

The linkage between sales at one end of the chain and wages at the other is so remote and tenuous that there is no assurance that a wage change will have the desired effect upon sales. In fact, it may produce no result at all or encourage the opposite from that sought. Hence it is impossible for the arbitrator who has decided that the firm needs wage relief to translate that conclusion into a precise figure. He must make a judgment that is largely subjective.

In concluding, we may recall the remark of the management representative that, although profit position seldom determines a wage offer directly, "it has a strong effect on our frame of mind." Much the same

---

[45] Arthur M. Ross, *Trade Union Wage Policy* (Berkeley: University of California Press, 1948), p. 90.

[46] Ross points out that this analysis does not apply to the exceptional industries in which piece-rate compensation prevails, labor cost is a substantial proportion of total cost, and overhead and materials are made to move in the same direction as wages. It is significant that the notable wage cuts agreed to by unions either in collective bargaining or by rigged arbitration have occurred in such industries—clothing, textiles, hosiery. *Ibid.*, pp. 91–92.

can be said of the employees, their union, and the arbitrator. If the company is making a lot of money, the labor organization is inclined to demand a bigger slice of the pie and the neutral to grant it. Conversely, if the employer is suffering a setback financially, the union tends to moderate its price and the arbitrator to be more sparing. This is a rephrasing of the American custom of sharing both prosperity and adversity. The tradition, however, hardly lends itself to mathematical measurement. As Pierson has pointed out in distinguishing between union demands that could and those that could not be afforded, "the dividing line had to be based, in the last analysis, on personal judgment."[47]

5. Differential Features of the Work

This title is phrased with sufficient broadness to embrace a variety of factors that affect wage rates. They include skill, hazard, onerousness, regularity of employment, intensiveness of effort, and the money value of nonrate fringes. These considerations, of course, are vital in wage administration. They lie at the root of internal rate structures, providing the rationale for differentials between jobs and premiums for unusual burdens of employment. Such factors, however, have little to do with general wage movements, the matter of concern here.

This is apparent in the fact that this criterion plays only a minor role in wage arbitration. Unions rarely cite it and neutrals virtually never give it decisive weight. Only employers refer to it with moderate frequency, in about one-tenth of their citations. This, normally, is part of an effort to detract from the union's more conventional justification of a wage increase. In the *Reading Street Railway* case, for example, the company argued strenuously that its fringes were superior to those on comparable properties and should be credited against wage rates.[48]

Arbitrators have had little difficulty in establishing a rule to cover this point. They hold that features of the work, though appropriate for fixing differentials between jobs, should not influence a general wage movement. As a consequence, in across-the-board wage cases, they have ignored claims that tractor-trailer drivers were entitled to a premium for physical strain; that fringe benefits should be charged off against wage rates; that offensive odors in a fish-reduction plant merited a differential; that weight should be given the fact that employees of a utility, generally speaking, were more skilled than workers in the community at large; that merit and experience deserved special recogni-

---

[47] Pittsburgh Railways Co. and Amalgamated Street Railway Employees, 17 *LA* 155 (1951).
[48] Reading Street Railway Co. and Amalgamated Street Railway Employees, 6 *LA* 860 (1947).

tion; and that regularity of employment should bar an otherwise justified increase.[49] Further, in the *New York Times* case Dunlop held that
the general increase should be effectuated so as not to disturb the rate
structure. "A salary increase by arbitration should provide a minimum
change in the salary structure negotiated by the parties. The relative
differentials in dollar terms among employees in the same group . . .
should likewise be generally preserved by the arbitrator."[50]

The theory behind this rule is that the parties accounted for these
factors in their past collective bargaining over rates. Hence established
differentials and premiums are regarded as fixed for purposes of general
wage changes. Such movements, in other words, are by definition across-
the-board in character, since the criteria that shape them affect all employees equally. The granting of differential adjustments, therefore,
would be inherently inequitable. Further, these factors are very hard
to measure. Those that directly affect individual rates and premiums,
for example, skill, experience, hazard, and onerousness, would draw
the arbitrator into the complex and tenuous area of job evaluation.
Some others—by way of illustration, a claim that employees in the unit
are more skilled than those in the community—are virtually impossible
to translate into cents per hour.

Occasionally, a case arises in which the arbitrator feels that the differential argument is so weighty that he must modify the rule. The
money consequence is that he grants a bit less than the amount supported by other wage-determining criteria. Two such cases were found.
In the Reading transit award, already referred to, the neutral stated that
the fringes were so favorable, though hardly yielding to precise measurement, that he could not completely ignore them.[51] In the *Public Service*
case the employer had unilaterally instituted a job evaluation plan, the
effect of which was an average increase of three cents per hour given
to all employees. The arbitration board ignored the plan in principle;
it granted, for example, an across-the-board adjustment that brought
some employees over the top of the rate ranges. It could not, however,
blink the fact of the three cents, and so "felt constrained to lower its

[49] D. C. Trucking Assn. and Teamsters, 1 *LA* 89 (1946); Georgia Power Co. and
Amalgamated Street Railway Employees, 4 *LA* 297 (1946); American Fisheries Co.
and Cannery Workers, 5 *LA* 220 (1946); Pacific Gas & Electric Co. and Utility Workers,
7 *LA* 528 (1947); New York City Omnibus Corp. and Transport Workers, 7 *LA* 794
(1947); R. H. Macy & Co. and Retail, Wholesale and Department Store Union, 9 *LA*
305 (1947); San Francisco Employers Council and Mine, Mill and Smelter Workers, 9
LA 401 (1948); *Detroit News* and Brotherhood of Electrical Workers, 12 *LA* 1110
(1949).
[50] *New York Times* and Newspaper Guild, 15 *LA* 333 (1950).
[51] Reading Street Railway Co. and Amalgamated Street Railway Employees, 6 *LA*
860 (1947).

sights on the amount of increase which considerations of cost of living and patterns . . . might otherwise justify."[52]

6. *Substandards of Living*

The concept behind this criterion is that workers and their families deserve a standard of life at least at the minimum level of health and decency. This factor has been variously described, for example, as "a level of adequate living," "a commonly accepted standard of living," "a fair wage," "an American standard," "a living wage." It is as much an ethical as an economic notion. As such, it is a particularly appropriate subject for legislation, and both the states and the federal government have responded with minimum-wage statutes.

The substandard criterion has had a long history in American wage determination. It came in for considerable attention in the latter part of the nineteenth and the early years of the present century as a result of research into poverty, the development of budget studies, and the emergence of state minimum-wage laws for women. At the time of World War I the government adopted it as a basic policy in wage-setting, notably by the National War Labor Board, the Shipbuilding Labor Adjustment Board, and the Anthracite Coal Commission of 1920. The vogue passed shortly thereafter, largely because of the postwar depression, and has never fully revived. The passage of the Fair Labor Standards Act in 1938, doubtless, was an important contributory factor to the decline of the criterion.

A generation ago the concept was usually called "the living wage" in contrast to such current terms as "substandards" or "worker's budgets." Words, like women's dress, reflect the shifting values of a society over time and this change in phraseology represents a gradual recognition that the economic deserves more attention than the ethical content of the criterion. The growth of the national income, with a consequent rise in the standard of life of American workers, has caused the problem of poverty to recede in importance. Citizens are more likely to become morally aroused over a wage of two dollars per week than over one of two dollars per hour.

Several agencies presently construct budgets that work their way into the wage cases. Although this is not the place to describe them in detail, a word about the more important ones is in order.[53] The Bureau of Labor Statistics' "City Worker's Family Budget" is the one most fre-

---

[52] Public Service Electric & Gas Co. and Chemical Workers, 12 *LA* 672 (1949).

[53] They are summarized in Jules Backman, *Economic Data Utilized in Wage Arbitration*, Labor Relations Series (Philadelphia: University of Pennsylvania Press, 1952), pp. 16–19. See also Lester S. Kellogg and Dorothy S. Brady, "The City Worker's Family Budget," *Monthly Labor Review*, 66 (February, 1948), 133–170.

quently cited. The BLS assumes a family of four, consisting of father, mother, and two children under fifteen. The father's wages constitute the sole source of income. The Bureau estimates the annual cost of "a modest but adequate standard of living" for this family. Expert technical advice helped to fix the required quantities of the components of the budget. The Bureau prices these goods and services in large cities. A formula for adjusting the results to other family sizes—two, three, and five persons—is offered.

The Heller Committee for Research in Social Economics of the University of California publishes four budgets annually for San Francisco: for the families of an executive, of a white-collar worker, of a wage earner, and of dependent families. The Heller worker's budget is pitched on a higher level of living than that of the BLS. A number of the states also make budgetary estimates, particularly in connection with their minimum wage laws for women. Finally, there have been studies on a noncontinuous basis, such as one by the Works Progress Administration in the 'thirties, by CIO unions late in the war, and by the Haynes Foundation for Los Angeles for a few recent years.

As might be expected, the substandard criterion is quite frequently referred to by unions, constituting about one-twelfth of their citations. Employers almost never invoke it and arbitrators are not far behind them in abstemiousness.

The typical arbitral view of the substandards criterion was expressed by Pierson in the *Restaurant-Hotel Employers* case:

> Except to indicate a general goal or direction which almost all groups in our economy have come to recognize, the Arbitrator can give little weight to the Joint Board's arguments regarding the importance of maintaining . . . adequate living standards; [this criterion] may well be [a] proper guide . . . for social policy but [it is] not much help in determining the specific amount by which employment standards should be increased or decreased in a case such as this.[54]

The reluctance of arbitrators to lend significant weight to this criterion rests upon a variety of objections. The first is that the result sup-

---

[54] Restaurant-Hotel Employers' Council of Southern California and Hotel and Restaurant Employees, 12 *LA* 1098 (1949). See also Atlantic & Gulf Coast Shippers and Maritime Union, 6 *LA* 700 (1947); California Street Cable Railway Co. and Amalgamated Street Railway Employees, 7 *LA* 91 (1947); Pacific Gas & Electric Co. and Utility Workers, 7 *LA* 528 (1947); Twin City Rapid Transit Co. and Amalgamated Street Railway Employees, 7 *LA* 845 (1947); Puget Sound Navigation Co. and Inland-boatmen, 8 *LA* 563 (1947); RKO Radio Pictures and Office and Professional Workers, 10 *LA* 550 (1948); Los Angeles Transit Lines and Amalgamated Street Railway Employees, 11 *LA* 118 (1948); Realty Advisory Board and Building Service Employees, 12 *LA* 352 (1949). A study of the wage decisions of emergency and arbitration boards in railroad cases reveals that the substandard criterion has never been given serious weight. Frederic Meyers, "Criteria in the Making of Wage Decisions by 'Neutrals': The Railroads as a Case Study," *Industrial and Labor Relations Review*, IV (April, 1951), 350.

ported by the budget may have little or no relevance to the money range of difference between the parties. Even the union's opening demand, recognized by everyone as excessive, is often below the substandard figure. In the *Restaurant-Hotel Employers* case, for example, the Haynes Foundation budget for Los Angeles justified an increase of at least two dollars and perhaps three dollars per day; yet the union had asked for only one dollar.[55]

The second reservation is with respect to the conception and construction of the budgets. Decisions as to what should or should not be included are inherently subjective. Should the family consume 10.1 or 15.1 or 20.1 quarts of ice cream each year? More important, is the intention of the budget to maintain these people at bare subsistence, at a somewhat superior level of health and decency, or at a still higher "American" standard of living, whatever that may be? The objective, obviously, will affect the result. Further, costs vary from locality to locality, rather less than most people assume between large cities in different regions and somewhat more than they think between big and small communities. The available budgets may not measure the community at issue. Finally, and this is a common criticism, the budget is constructed about a synthetic family which seldom comports with reality. It assumes, for example, that the father is the only breadwinner, whereas mothers often work full or part time and even children may have some income. The notion that a family of four is typical is particularly vulnerable, as the BLS recognizes by offering alternative formulas. The 1950 Census, for example, reveals that only 18.1 per cent of households consist of four persons; 60.7 per cent have fewer and 21.2 per cent have more members. The average family size in the bargaining unit in question may differ significantly from that used in the budget.[56] Finally, the normal distribution by family size among a group of wage earners is so great as to sap the average of meaning for the purpose of wage determination.

The third criticism is that the national income is not large enough to accommodate a distribution to all recipients at the budget level. Or, phrased another way, if at one moment all members of the labor force were given a dollar income sufficient to purchase the items in the BLS budget, there would not be enough goods and services to go around. Hence prices would rise and there would be no net gain in aggregate

[55] Restaurant-Hotel Employers' Council of Southern California and Hotel and Restaurant Employees, 12 *LA* 1091 (1949). See also Puget Sound Navigation Co. and Inlandboatmen, 8 *LA* 563 (1947); Los Angeles Transit Lines and Amalgamated Street Railway Employees, 11 *LA* 118 (1948); Realty Advisory Board and Building Service Employees, 12 *LA* 352 (1949).

[56] See Realty Advisory Board and Building Service Employees, 12 *LA* 352 (1949).

real income. In the past this was a basic objection of those who supported the living-wage principle as a matter of social policy.[57] More recently, Slichter has pointed out that if all workers received an income adequate to buy the components of the Heller budget, the economy would need to produce 60 per cent more consumer goods than it actually turned out.[58] Historically, this result is a function of the relationship between the rate of growth of the labor force and that of the national income. Of late, the latter has been expanding more rapidly than the former. If this trend continues, the time may not be far distant when the national income actually will permit a distribution at the budget level.

The fourth objection is the difficulty of translating a budget estimate into a specific wage adjustment. Even assuming that the budget figure were precise—and we know how rough an approximation it is—there is a serious statistical impediment to its conversion into wage rates. The budgets are constructed upon an annual basis, whereas almost none of the workers to whom they are applied are paid for so long a term. The great majority are hourly-rated and virtually all the others receive income by the week or the month. Obviously, the number of hours, weeks, or months worked will influence annual take-home. Many wage earners are subject to layoff or are afforded the opportunity to work overtime at premium rates. How are these fluctuating circumstances to be predicted? How are they to be averaged for all employees in the unit in face of widely varying work-time effects upon annual income?

The final disadvantage of the substandards criterion is that its logic is economy-wide, while its application is sought for a particular firm or group of firms. The individual employer, therefore, can argue forcefully that he is the subject of discrimination. If a budget-supported standard of life justifies a given minimum income, all those below it have an equal right to its enjoyment. Hence it should be enforced generally rather than differentially.

These objections, then, constitute the grounds for the unwillingness of arbitrators to accord the substandard factor serious weight in wage cases. They do not, however, justify its exclusion from wage determination. This is evident in the fact that American society has supported minimum-wage statutes to protect those at the bottom of the income scale. The great majority of workers are above these minima; hence wage disputes are nearly always at a suprastatutory level. Occasionally, an

---

[57] Paul H. Douglas, "Factors in Wage Determination," *American Economic Review*, Supp., XIII (March, 1923), 141.

[58] Sumner H. Slichter, *Basic Criteria Used in Wage Negotiations* (Chicago: Chicago Assn. of Commerce, 1947), pp. 10–14. See also Twin City Rapid Transit Co. and Amalgamated Street Railway Employees, 7 *LA* 845 (1947).

arbitrator is called upon to deal with rates so low that the substandards criterion is appropriate. This was true in the *San Francisco Hospital* case, where none of the employees received in excess of $122.50 per month based upon a forty-eight hour work week and the institutions were outside the jurisdiction of the Fair Labor Standards Act. The majority of the arbitration board, therefore, sought "a fair and living wage" and ignored the fact that cost of living did not justify so large an increase. It is significant that no reference was made to the budgets, which would have supported an increase far beyond the limits of acceptability.[59]

7. *Productivity*

No wage-determining factor has provoked so much fanciful thinking, rudimentary misunderstanding, and frustrated hope as productivity. Since the secular trend of man-hour output has been upward, unions have sought to exploit this fact as a basis for wage advance and many managements have looked on it with suspicion. On both sides the conclusion has as often been grounded upon visceral as upon cerebral processes. It is, no doubt, significant that all parties—the government, the labor movement, organized industry, and even the economists—are in accord at the level of principle that rising productivity is a valid justification for higher wages. Such unanimity on the part of groups with obviously divergent interests evokes suspicion on its face. It suggests that they may be talking about different things and that a little defining is in order at the outset.

From the standpoint of wage determination, the productivity concept is applied to two quite different factors: first, greater output resulting from more intensive effort by the worker and, second, higher output stemming from general economic and social forces. The origin of the former is in the individual; he works harder, faster, more skillfully. The latter is beyond his control since its sources are the broad determinants of a progressive economy. The first factor is the basis for the piece-rate system of wage payment and is often measurable by simply counting the number of units turned out by the worker or a small group of workers. Because it is related to individual effort, it is not a criterion that shapes general wage movements. Hence it will be excluded from consideration here. This distinction, however, has not been uniformly made by unions or management, to say nothing of an occasional arbitrator.[60]

[59] San Francisco Hospital Conference and Hospital and Institutional Workers, 5 *LA* 137 (1946).

[60] Woytinsky, *op. cit.,* p. 116; Manufacturers' Protective Assn. and Stove Mounters, 13 *LA* 900 (1949); Public Service Electric & Gas Co. and Brotherhood of Electrical Workers, 15 *LA* 496 (1950).

The second concept of productivity is both more subtle and less susceptible to measurement. In most general terms, productivity is a comparison between production (in specific units) and one, several, or all of the factors employed in production (in specific units). The productivity of any of the following may be measured: capital equipment, fuel, materials, labor. Our concern, of course, is with the last. Labor productivity is a statistic showing the relationship between the input of labor measured in man-hours and the output of the economy or industry or plant measured in dollars or in physical units. When output is expressed in money terms, the series is deflated to dollars of constant value. This essay in definition leads directly to the methods of measurement.

Two basic techniques are used, the first being the gross national product approach of the Department of Commerce. Here the value of the total output of the private sector of the economy is deflated and compared with the total input of man-hours. The second method measures changes in the quantity of labor needed to produce a standardized physical unit of end product at different time intervals. It is used by the Bureau of Labor Statistics on an industry-by-industry basis. It can be applied, however, only to a fraction of the economy. Some industries must be excluded because their products are not sufficiently homogeneous from year to year; others because data on man-hour input are lacking; and still others because the method is wholly inappropriate, for example, in the services, trade, construction, and government.

The sponsors of both methods are in agreement on the long-run trend, namely, that it is upward. The Department of Commerce estimates that the rate of growth averages 2.1 per cent annually. The BLS concludes that the rise is about 3 per cent for the manufacturing industries it surveys and that 2 per cent is not an unreasonable figure for the whole economy.

The causes of productivity changes are both long and short term. The former comprise the progressive secular forces at work in the economy: advancing research and development, improved technology, more efficient methods, better management, accumulated labor know-how, labor-management coöperation. The short-run influences include the load factor and overstrain of resources. Load is particularly important in the utilities and transportation. Here a virtually constant input of man-hours will result in widely varying levels of output as a function of the demand for the service. Wartime is an illustration of excessive strain. Its pressures call into play outmoded equipment, marginal workers, and poor materials with a consequent decline in productivity.

Perhaps the best estimate of change that we possess is the approximately 2 per cent annual average rise in real output per man-hour for the whole economy upon which the General Motors annual improvement factor rests. A leading expert has observed of even this estimate:

Such a figure can be derived only from deflated national income series that are rough approximations prior to 1919, if not 1929; rough estimates of employment that are based on incomplete payroll statistics with gaps filled in from the Censuses of Occupations adjusted for unemployment; and very crude estimates of change in the length of the work week. No one familiar with the basic data and their limitations would call the final estimate precise. He would prefer to speak of a range, say of 1.6 to 2.2 per cent per annum.[61]

One may conclude that productivity as a wage-determining standard leaves something to be desired on grounds of precision. The fact that the expert has hesitated to place his foot in the quicksand, however, has not invariably deterred the innocent.

This has notably been the case in recent years when the productivity argument has become quite fashionable. It has obtained general support from labor unions and from some employers. The turning event, undoubtedly, was the decision by General Motors and the United Automobile Workers in 1948 to incorporate the improvement factor in their collective agreement. It has since spread to the remainder of automobile manufacturing and industries peripheral to it as well as to unrelated firms that deal with the auto union. The prolonged debate over productivity wage policy within the Wage Stabilization Board in 1951–1952, though fruitless as to concrete program, provided further momentum. The basic railroad wage decision of 1953 is another important step.

Despite these developments, the productivity criterion has hardly penetrated the crust of wage arbitration. Only 2.4 per cent of the citations in our sample were related to this factor, and arbitrators never gave it decisive weight. Emergency boards and arbitrators in the railroad industry before 1953 appear to have been no more impressed with the productivity argument.[62]

This arbitral abstemiousness stems from the unusual difficulties that obstruct the application of this criterion to the cases. The statistical manipulations that go on, though impressive for their quantity and ingenuity, are not marked for their translatability into cents per hour. As a management man who favored linking wages to productivity has observed, "We have been talking about it, but we haven't been able to

---

[61] Solomon Fabricant, "Productivity Measurement," *Proceedings of New York University Third Annual Conference on Labor* (Albany: Bender, 1950), p. 83.
[62] Meyers, *op. cit.*, p. 351.

work out any sound plan for this industry."[63] There are several impediments that invite examination.

The first, already suggested for the national estimate, is the formidable problem of measurement in the particular dispute. It is always difficult and sometimes impossible to determine the rate of productivity change for the individual plant. In addition, most managements and unions are lacking in the technical competence to do so. Even when they try, the arbitrator is inclined to cast a wary eye upon their results.[64] Further, all the published productivity series describe the past, at best being a year late. Hence their usefulness for the present, to say nothing of the future, is no better than indirect. Since the arbitrator must fix a prospective wage, his reliance upon this criterion calls for high competence in prognostication.

The second obstacle to applying productivity in wage determination is the distortion effect. The familiar 2 per cent economy-wide estimate is deceptively comforting in its simplicity. Actually, the dispersion among industries is considerable; some advance at a higher rate, some at the same rate, some at a lower rate, and some decline. There is a similar scattering about the average among firms in the same industry and among departments of the same company. Even the figure for the whole economy is misleading within short time spans. It is, in fact, a long-run average with wide intermediate fluctuations. The significant interval, therefore, may bear no relationship to 2 per cent. The general implication of these qualifications is that the linkage of wages to productivity in the industry, firm, or department would create monstrous inequities in the wage structure with resulting chaos in labor-management relations. "To tie wages rigidly in each minor segment of the economy to changes in physical productivity in that segment," Kerr has noted, "would . . . cause greater distortion as between and among progressive, static and regressive industries than could be sustained."[65] The logic of this criterion for wage policy, rather, is equal treatment of all industries, all firms, all departments without regard to their individual performances on productivity.[66]

The third limitation is the total absence of a formula for allocating the gains of rising productivity among the claimants. Consumers argue for lower prices, workers for higher wages, management for higher salaries, and investors for fatter dividends. Few issues stir professional

---

[63] Quoted in Woytinsky, *op. cit.,* p. 115.

[64] San Diego Gas & Electric Co. and Brotherhood of Electrical Workers, 12 *LA* 245 (1949); Manufacturers' Protective Assn. and Stove Mounters, 13 *LA* 900 (1949).

[65] Pacific Gas & Electric Co. and Utility Workers, 7 *LA* 530 (1947).

[66] Indianapolis Railways and Amalgamated Street Railway Employees, 9 *LA* 319 (1947).

economists to such dissension as the contest between proponents of disbursing the gains in lower prices as against higher wages. Soule pointed out sensibly many years ago: "As exercises in the realm of morals such speculations may possibly be useful, but as guides to the proper distribution of the product they are quite without meaning, because they are not subject to scientific analysis and quantitative measurement in a living economic world."[67]

The final shortcoming—primarily a union problem—stems from the fact that productivity sometimes declines. This is not infrequent with the individual firm, for example, a mine approaching the exhaustion of its ore body. It also occurs to the national average in short time periods, by way of illustration, the years immediately following World War II. Is this criterion a two-way street? Shall wages be permitted to fall as well as rise? The absence of a formula for precise allocation among the claimants serves to protect workers against carrying the burden of productivity declines. An arbitrator, for example, refused to deny employees a cost-of-living increase because he could not separate out their responsibility for a drop in the efficiency of the industry.[68]

In conclusion, the productivity criterion, despite the interest it has evoked, has played a subordinate role in wage arbitration. This is not because the factor is unrelated to wage determination; in fact, it is the underlying cause of real wage advance, of the long-term rise in the standard of life of the American people. Rather, this neglect stems primarily from the extraordinary measurement difficulties that confront the parties and the arbitrator in applying productivity to the particular wage dispute. A further negative consideration is that most arbitrators, like most unions and employers, lack the statistical sophistication to deal effectively with productivity data. The impediments to administering this criterion on an individual plant or industry basis suggest that the only workable application is of the economy-wide average to all units. In this connection, it is significant that General Motors has led the way in doing so, since it is the largest of our manufacturing operations with branches throughout the nation. If firms or industries of a related order of magnitude continue to adopt the GM example, productivity may rise in importance in wage arbitration. This is not because these units will arbitrate (they probably will not), but because the principle will be so widely accepted that many small and medium-sized companies will follow in their wake. In such cases the arbitrator will not base his decision on productivity, but rather on the comparison.

---

[67] George Soule, "The Productivity Factor in Wage Determinations," *American Economic Review*, Supp., XIII (March, 1923), 129. See also Pacific Gas & Electric Co. and Utility Workers, 7 *LA* 528 (1947).

[68] Associated General Contractors and Operating Engineers, 9 *LA* 201 (1947).

8. *Miscellaneous Criteria*

Productivity was the last of the major criteria of wage determination. Four standards of a lower order of importance remain to be considered: the hours-of-work factor, general economic considerations, union behavior, and manpower attraction. Each will be briefly discussed.

a. *Hours-of-work factor.* The basic hours issue—the length of the work day and of the work week—is not a wage matter at all. Hence it is of no concern to us here. The majority of workers, however, receive earnings (daily, weekly, annual) in accordance with a formula that includes the time factor: number of hours worked multiplied by the hourly rate. As a result, the question of hours occasionally slips in among the wage criteria. The arbitration cases supply a number of illustrations.

A widely observed principle of wage administration is that regularity of employment shall affect the hourly rate. Perhaps the most notable example occurs in the building trades scales. Craftsmen employed in construction, who suffer sharp fluctuations in employment, customarily receive higher rates than men with the same skills employed by utilities, who work steadily. As a result, unions sometimes urge higher wages on the grounds of uncertain employment and employers argue for lower rates because work is steady. Occasionally an arbitrator is inclined to give secondary weight to one of these contentions. In the postwar New York longshore dispute, for example, Davis did not hesitate to award the high rate justified by cost of living, because he recognized that the dockers were normally out of work one-third of the time.[69]

A further intrusion of hours into the wage area occurs when the employer eliminates regular overtime. Employees accustomed to high weekly earnings based in part upon premium hours often insist upon a rate increase when the work week is shortened. This, of course, was the union claim for the maintenance of forty-eight hour wartime take-home when the work week reverted to forty hours after V-J Day. The fact-finding boards that considered this issue at the time were inclined to give heavy weight to the union argument.[70]

Several arbitrators have been called upon to face the same question and have come up with quite different results. One position is represented by the *Roberts Pressure Valve* case. The employers had just cut the overtime out of a regular forty-five hour week. Singer decided:

> The union has made much of the fact that the employees in effect have sustained a reduction in wages by the loss of overtime. An employer cannot guarantee the

---

[69] New York Shipping Assn. and Longshoremen, 1 *LA* 80 (1945). See also Reading Street Railway Co. and Amalgamated Street Railway Employees, 6 *LA* 860 (1947).

[70] See, for example, General Motors Corp. and Automobile Workers, 1 *LA* 125 (1946).

maintenance of take-home-pay. If business does not warrant the continuation of overtime and the premium pay that flows therefrom, the employers should be able to cease such an operation. This is truly a function of management, and no union should be permitted to thrust upon the employer its opinions regarding managerial policy. I do not take as a criterion in ascertaining an increase, the maintenance of take-home-pay which is based on premium pay.[71]

An arbitration board in the *Woolworth* case held precisely the opposite in face of a claim for higher rates based on the employer's elimination of eight hours of overtime.

> This might not be a critically important factor standing alone. It becomes important, however, because the formerly steady opportunity to earn additional wages for overtime work was apparently a positive influence in shaping the pattern of straight-time rates. In a realistic, though perhaps not a technical sense, overtime earnings had become an integral part of the wage structure.[72]

At what point does regular overtime become integrated with the rate structure? The arbitrators offered no clue.

A variation of this problem arises when the initiative in dispensing with steady overtime comes from the union rather than from the employer. In such a case the arbitrator ruled that the refusal of the employees to work premium hours constituted a bar to a claim for higher wages based upon lower weekly earnings.[73]

A final take-home question concerns a reduction in the work week concurrent with a rise in living costs. Shall the hourly rates be fixed in money or real terms? This was the issue in the *Columbia University* case, in which the parties agreed to drop from forty-four to forty hours with the same take-home. Meyer then faced the question of the resulting real wage.

> If it is lower the workers will not have secured the full benefits of a reduced workweek. On the contrary, their standard of living will have been impaired, and they will pay in diminished purchasing power for their diminished hours of work. A reduction of four hours in the workweek is an important advantage to labor. It may be deemed a sufficient betterment of working conditions to take the place of a betterment of real take-home pay. But it does not appear to me, either in quantity or quality, the sort of gain which would presently justify an actual loss in real weekly wages.[74]

Hence he awarded the employees the same real take-home that they enjoyed when they worked forty-four hours.

b. *General economic considerations.* Occasionally the parties to a wage dispute advance arguments that reflect their broad views of eco-

---

[71] Roberts Pressure Valve Co. and Architects, Engineers, Chemists and Technicians, 8 *LA* 667 (1947).

[72] F. W. Woolworth Co. and Retail, Wholesale and Department Store Employees, 4 *LA* 506 (1946).

[73] Insuline Corp. and Machinists, 4 *LA* 308 (1946).

[74] Columbia University and Transport Workers, 5 *LA* 312 (1946).

nomic society rather than the particular matters at issue. On the union side this usually takes the form of the purchasing-power theory. The labor member of an arbitration board framed it in this fashion:

> The Union has shown . . . that the material progress of this country is bound up with the purchasing power of its wage earners. Its prosperity depends on the continued expansion of its industry and agriculture, and they in turn depend on the existence of an expanding consumers' market able to absorb those products at prevailing prices. The bulk of consumers are wage earners and unless their purchasing power expands steadily, the economic progress of the country will be interrupted.[75]

Employers counter at the same level with the contention that wage increases are inherently inflationary and so dangerous to the public welfare. This is "the vicious spiral" with labor costs serving as the initiator of evil: higher wages cause rising unit costs which force prices up.[76] Whatever force this argument may have, obviously, is related to the direction in which the price structure is moving. In a sense, each position is a rather imprecise restatement of the productivity and financial-adversity criteria.

The fact that arbitrators never give either serious weight suggests that they function primarily as window dressing rather than as wage-fixing tools. Their shortcomings as wage criteria are patent on several counts. First, individual bargains, excepting a handful, cover only fragments of the economy. Hence their potential for either enlarging national consumption or forcing the general price level upward is negligible. Second, both theories open themselves to the charge of oversimplification since the relationship of wages to aggregate demand and prices is neither direct nor simple. That is, the wage rate is only one among several factors that determine the volume of consumption and that influence the structure of prices. Third, these arguments may be totally unrelated to the dispute at hand. In the southern California *Restaurant-Hotel Employers* case, for example, the purchasing power theory might have supported an increase of $3.00 per day; yet, the union's demand, fixing the outer limit of the arbitrator's discretion, was for only $1.00.[77] Finally, these contentions deal with conjecture rather than with reality. Framed another way, they tax the arbitrator's skill at prognosis rather than his talent for analysis.[78]

---

[75] Capital Transit Co. and Amalgamated Street Railway Employees, 9 *LA* 696 (1947).

[76] New York City Omnibus Corp. and Transport Workers, 7 *LA* 794 (1947).

[77] Restaurant-Hotel Employers' Council of Southern California and Hotel and Restaurant Employees, 12 *LA* 1091 (1949).

[78] In this connection the dissenting opinion of the labor member of a board issued on the eve of the great economic expansion that accompanied the outbreak of the Korean War makes amusing retrospective reading: "Unemployment is steadily increasing. There is no prospect that business activities will increase in 1950 to restore full employment. . . . If this trend is to be reversed and general business activities main-

In the *Pacific Gas & Electric* case the parties advanced both arguments: wages as income in the purchasing-power theory and wages as cost in the inflation contention. Kerr's disposition of these matters supplies an appropriate note on which to close.

> Wages are, of course, both costs and income. A full picture of the coin is not obtained by viewing only one side. Economists do not yet agree whether the cost and income aspects of wages offset each other, or on the circumstances under which one or the other aspect is the more important. Were it entirely clear, still the disposition of this present case, coming as it does late in the "second round," could not conceivably impel the national economy down the high road of inflation or the low road of depression. Strongly as the parties may feel individually about wages-as-costs or wages-as-income, this is not the tribunal in which an effective decision can be made either way. The effects on inflation or depression cannot be a controlling consideration in this case. Were there a clear national policy on wages setting forth the public interest in wage changes, or were this a "wage leadership" case more attention might be paid to these public welfare arguments.[79]

c. *Union behavior*. This strange and, fortunately, infrequent argument is that the union's strike record, good or bad, should influence the wage decision. The street railway employees' organization in Lorain, Ohio, for example, urged the arbitrator to give weight in a wage case to the absence of work stoppages. The union, it not immodestly declared, is "entitled to special commendation," particularly when the fact is noted that Lorain is "dominated by an aggressive labor organization employed by a dominant steel company, and strikes are not uncommon."[80] The Waterfront Employers turned the coin over, urging the neutral to deny an increase because the union had engaged in numerous job actions and contract violations. Miller disposed of the argument in that case and, the writer hopes, in all others in this fashion:

> Over the past, strikes, lock-outs, and short-lived arbitrators have characterized the relations of the parties. But, in directing attention in this interim wage proceeding to the Union's contribution to this unenviable record, the employers misconceive the remedy. The roots of these difficulties lie deep in the whole pattern of the past relationship of the parties and the remedy for their failures in collective bargaining, whatever it may be, lies elsewhere than in a punitive denial of a cost of living wage adjustment.[81]

---

tained or improved, wage increases must be given by all employers who are in a position to do so without raising prices, thus creating new buying power and demand for industrial products, so that production and employment will rise. The alternative is increasing unemployment with concomitant decreasing purchasing power and another business depression." United Press Assns. and Commercial Telegraphers, 14 *LA* 868 (1950).

[79] Pacific Gas & Electric Co. and Utility Workers, 7 *LA* 531 (1947).

[80] Employees Transit Lines and Amalgamated Street Railway Employees, 4 *LA* 749 (1946).

[81] Waterfront Employers Assn. and Longshoremen and Warehousemen, 9 *LA* 178 (1947).

The union's behavior, like the employer's, is as irrelevant to wage determination as a ball player's language, good or bad, would be to his qualifications as a pitcher.

d. *Manpower attraction.* The final criterion of wage determination is advanced only by employers. On rare occasions they argue that an increase should be denied because the firm is able to recruit an adequate labor force at the existing level of wages. An employer member of an arbitration board put it this way:

> The Company demonstrated conclusively that it has been able, at all times, to attract all of the employees that it needed, and, that once employed such employees tend to remain with the Company for long periods of time unless removed for cause. Therefore, no increase in wage rates is needed to attract and hold employees.[52]

Only one arbitrator has dealt explicitly with this contention, although the silence of others has constituted rejection. Simkin, in the *Reading Street Railway* case, recognized that the employer could recruit at the existing scale, in fact, that all war veterans had voluntarily resumed their old jobs. Nevertheless, he ruled that "the fact that employees will remain in a relatively low-paid industry is not in itself any sound reason for denying them a fair wage."[53] His notions of "fairness" in the circumstances of that dispute depended primarily upon the employees' claims of intraindustry and interindustry comparisons and cost of living.

Beyond equity, there are several additional objections to the manpower standard. First, as framed by employers, it is exclusively negative; it does not permit wages to rise. Second, even if turned around in a rising market, there is no way to translate the recruitment factor precisely into cents per hour. Finally, if this criterion were generally accepted, it would create wage inequities and undermine those elements of rationality that the wage structure presently exhibits. Within the plant, for example, the availability of manpower might permit the elimination of differentials between skilled and unskilled workmen. Wide rate distortions between firms in the same industry would emerge because some were located in communities with tight and others in towns with loose labor markets.[54]

---

[52] Birmingham Electric Co. and Amalgamated Street Railway Employees, 7 *LA* 835 (1947). See also Mason Contractors' Assn. of Detroit and Bricklayers, 12 *LA* 909 (1949).

[53] Reading Street Railway Co. and Amalgamated Street Railway Employees, 6 *LA* 868 (1947).

[54] Lester's studies reveal that competition between employers in the same labor market for the same grade of labor produces, not a "prevailing wage," but, rather, a dispersion of rates. Richard A. Lester, "Wage Diversity and Its Theoretical Implications," *Review of Economic Statistics*, XXVIII (August, 1946), 158.

VI. CONCLUSIONS

I

NEITHER American industry nor American labor has accepted the arbitration of general wage changes widely or permanently. Although its employment has grown secularly since the Civil War, the expansion has been sporadic. In periods of rapid price advance, notably during and after great wars, it has gained wide use. At times of price stability the procedure has won little favor.

To understand wage arbitration, one must take account of three basic considerations. The first is that it serves as a dependent variable of collective bargaining as practiced in the United States. Viewed from the vantage point of bargaining, the arbitrator plays a dual role in substitution. With regard to substance, his judgment replaces that of the parties in framing the wage fraction of the collective agreement; with respect to function, he substitutes for the work stoppage. As a consequence, he is under pressure to behave as they would have acted if they had not needed him. He must strive, for example, to make his award acceptable, to avoid provoking a strike or lockout.

The second consideration is that the decision of a union and an employer to arbitrate wages is an exercise in strategy rather than a conflict over goals. The objective—from which neither side ever removes its eye—is the wage. They may employ various means to achieve it: agreement, strike, or arbitration. In the rare case in which they jointly elect the last, each has reluctantly concluded that it can gain its own vision of the wage no more effectively by the other devices.

The final generalization is that the criteria of wage determination are something less than definitive. Their shortcomings are as hazardous to the arbitrator as they are to the parties. His problem is not to lay out a yardstick and measure off an amount, but, rather, to balance contesting standards in an exercise in responsible judgment.

This discussion has suggested that wage arbitration plays a secondary role in collective bargaining. There is, in fact, no risk in stating that not more than 2 per cent of general wage changes in peacetime are arbitrated.

The distribution of this fraction, however, is significant. The industries that employ it are primarily the public utilities, notably urban transit, and others that deal directly with the public, for example, retail trade. This is because unions and employers in these fields hesitate to antagonize the community with work stoppages. The great majority of mining and manufacturing firms, by contrast, seldom arbitrate wages.

As a matter of fact, almost no very large enterprises do so. Unions, apparently, are attracted to this procedure when they are weak, either internally so or by virtue of limitations on their exercise of the strike weapon. The practice of wage arbitration is concentrated in two geographical regions, the Atlantic and Pacific coasts, with very little in between or below.

Arbitrators' wage awards tend to come out somewhere between the positions of the parties. This is suggested by the fact that employer and union members of tripartite boards dissent with approximately equal frequency. It is confirmed by the money distribution of awards between union demands and company offers, which show that arbitrators rarely vote wholly with one side or the other. Much more often the decision is found roughly midway between them. It is not unreasonable to assume that both parties, by taking their positions, have discounted this result, thereby helping to produce it.

The criteria of wage determination are given sharply differing weights by the parties and arbitrators in the cases. Comparisons, by far, are the most important, normally intraindustry and less often interindustry. Arbitrators place greatest reliance upon the former and unions upon the latter. The second ranking standard is cost of living, again espoused warmly by arbitrators and with reserve by employers. The financial condition of the firm comes much further down the list and is, of course, primarily a management argument. All the remaining criteria together (differential features of the work, substandards, productivity, etc.) constitute a negligible fraction of the total. Hence wage arbitration revolves almost entirely about comparisons, cost of living, and the employer's profit situation.

Procedurally considered, the arbitration of wages is much like that of grievances with a few notable exceptions. An important one is the reopening clause, the key problem being the scope of the arbitrator's authority when wages are before him under an interim reopening rather than a new contract. Many neutrals, in the face of union opposition, have adopted the "erosion theory," that is, with reopening employees are entitled only to recompense for that fragment of wages that has deteriorated since the original negotiation of the agreement. The effect of this rule is to constrict the arbitrator's discretion almost exclusively to the cost-of-living criterion. A second procedural matter concerns the submission agreement. Should it specify wage standards, avoid them, or fix a range in cents per hour? The first two alternatives are deficient on grounds of difficulty of application and of risk to the parties; the last, however, has much to commend it. Third, the tripartite board form is particularly adapted to wage cases because it fosters the acceptability of the award, permits a freer flow of information between arbitrator and parties, and maximizes the possibility of settlement. Finally, arbitration can be politically useful in the administration of a wage cut. That is, a responsible union leader, who recognizes the necessity for a reduction, can shift the onus to an arbitrator, thereby maintaining stability within his organization. This may evolve into a "rigged case."

The criteria of wage determination are the tools for the fixing of wages. The most important, as already noted, is the comparison. In part, this is because it satisfies the powerful force of equity between individuals or groups that compete with one another. In addition, all the parties involved in a wage change derive some benefit from it: worker, union, employer, arbitrator. Finally, wage-setting by comparison permits ready translatability into cents per hour.

The intraindustry comparison is the most persuasive. In fact, arbitrators almost invariably subscribe to the principle of wage parity between firms in an industry. When this criterion comes into conflict with others, usually a plea of financial adversity, the intraindustry comparison prevails. Certain types of cases, however, are outside its application—those involving industry-wide bargaining and the wage leader. This is because neither provides a base unit for comparative purposes.

The execution of the parity principle to those situations to which it is applicable is beset with difficulties. Since industrial classifications are inherently arbitrary, it is often hard to define the borders of an industry. A further difficulty resides in the geography of the rate: shall the comparison encompass the locality, the metropolitan area, the region, the nation? Another problem arises when the operational or ownership patterns of competing firms differ. Again, should comparability be restricted to firms which sell in competition or may those in related lines be admitted? There are also several worker-oriented difficulties: differences in the content of jobs, in the methods of wage payment, in the regularity of employment, and in fringe benefits. In resolving these problems, arbitrators rely most heavily upon wage history. If the parties have in the past instituted wage changes in the same amount and at the same time as the base unit, neutrals are reluctant to disrupt the tandem. Faced with the opposite facts, they tend to reach the reverse conclusion.

The interindustry comparison, though often argued, rarely wins conclusive weight. There are a variety of reasons: differences between industries in product market, productivity, and profitability; and noncomparability with respect to job content, regularity of employment, and fringe benefits. There are several limited situations to which the interindustry comparison is sometimes applied, for example, as a check against the general wage trend, in a seller's product market, and under industry-wide bargaining. The remaining comparisons—intracompany, intraunion, and interunion—rarely arise and are applicable only to special situations. The last is the most important and is a consequence of either rival or contiguous unionism. In the face of jurisdictional conflict between labor organizations, arbitrators have little alternative but to rely on the principle of wage parity.

The second wage criterion in point of importance is cost of living. Its incidence is a function of the rate of change in the level of consumer prices. Its validity rests upon the ethical notion that the real wages of workers should not be depreciated by price movements beyond their control. Like the comparison, cost of living can be quickly converted into cents per hour. This standard raises several administrative problems, of which base date is most critical since it offers an open field for manipulation. The usual arbitral rule is to employ as base for computing cost-of-living adjustments the effective date of the prior contract. A second difficulty arises in the case of incentive systems or overtime earnings. Here arbitrators exclude these variables from the calculation. Neutrals, with some exceptions, give greater weight to cost of living than to a plea of financial hardship on the part of the employer. Arbitrators are more reluctant to cut wages when prices fall than they are to raise wages when prices rise.

The third criterion is financial condition of the employer, by which is meant affirmative ability to pay, inability to pay in face of a threat to survival, and, most commonly, unsatisfactory business conditions. Unlike the first two, this standard presents virtually insurmountable hurdles to a precise measurement and translation into cents per hour. For this and other reasons arbitrators seldom give a plea of financial hardship decisive weight. On the other hand, they do not often ignore it completely. More frequently, neutrals conclude that another criterion should generate the direction of the wage movement but that demonstrable financial adversity should limit the amount. This is another way of saying that the comparison and cost of living usually carry more weight. Further, arbitrators refuse to accept the argument of transit companies that a wage increase should be made contingent upon approval of a fare increase by a public utility commission. In the rare cases in which unions argue for higher wages based on large profits neutrals are unpersuaded.

The fourth standard is differential features of the work, including such factors as skill, hazard, onerousness, regularity of employment, effort, and the money value of fringes. These matters are vital to wage administration within the firm but play almost no role in general wage changes. Hence arbitrators have normally ignored the differential argument.

The fifth criterion is substandards, that is, that workers' families deserve a standard of life no lower than the minimum level of health and decency. Unions have so argued for many years, pointing to BLS and other budget studies. Recently arbitrators have not given this contention significant weight for a variety of reasons: the frequent irrelevance of the budget standard to the money range of difference between the parties; deficiencies in the conception and construction of the budgets when used for this purpose; the inability of the national income to accommodate a distribution to all recipients at the budget level; impediments to translation into cents per hour; and the unrelatedness of the argument to the employer at issue. There are rare cases, however, in which the extreme lowness of rates causes the arbitrator to go beyond comparisons and cost of living.

The sixth standard is productivity, certainly the most elusive and misunderstood of the lot. The fact that man-hour output has increased secularly has permitted a long-term rise in real wages. The application of this fact to particular cases, however, is fraught with difficulties. Of these, the gross inadequacy of the yardstick for wage-determining purposes is most important. Another obstacle is the distortion effect, the national average being a compound of widely varying rates of productivity advance. A further limitation is the absence of a formula for allocating gains among the claimants—consumers, workers, investors. As a result, arbitrators rarely give weight to productivity in the wage cases.

Finally, there remain a miscellany of minor criteria which only occasionally crop up in the arbitration awards. The hours-of-work factor arises in several forms. One is that regularity or intermittency of employment should affect a general wage change. Arbitrators never regard it as controlling but infrequently accord it secondary consideration. Another hours matter concerns the maintenance of weekly take-home in face of a reduction in the length of the work week, an issue of importance following the termination of World War II. Arbitral decisions diverge widely on this question. A second minor criterion consists of general economic arguments, such as the purchasing-power theory and the inflationary impact of wage increases. Arbitrators never give them decisive weight. A third standard is union behavior, that is, that the union's strike record, good or bad, should affect the wage award. Arbitrators, needless to say, are not impressed. The final miscellaneous standard is manpower attraction, an employer argument that a wage increase should be denied because the firm can recruit labor at existing rates. It conveys little force with neutrals.

II

The Webbs report the lament of Judge Ellison in the Yorkshire coal arbitration of 1879: "On what principle I have to deal with it I have not the slightest idea. . . . There is no principle of political economy involved in it. Both masters and men are arguing and standing upon what is completely within their rights."[1] Little notable progress has been made since. Confronted by a tough wage issue in the textile industry almost seventy years later, Brown admitted, "The plain fact of the matter is that, as economists or as citizens, we are woefully ignorant with respect to these questions."[2]

The arbitrator, therefore, must deal with wages outside the range of the theoretical systems. As W. P. Reeves, writing out of Australasian experience many years ago, noted: "The business of the labour arbitrator is not to please orthodox professors of economy, but rather to find a reasonable *modus vivendi* for two disputants who are unable to find it for themselves."[3] Hence the wage arbitrator shuns theory, not because it may be inadequate, but rather because he is under compulsions of a different order. He must be concerned with the immediate, the explicit, the pragmatic; he must award an amount in cents that will stick and thereby avoid a stoppage. At best, the arbitrator has no more than a long-run preoccupation with the long run.

In the wage area, as in collective bargaining generally, rationality is neither invariably present nor desirable. "Economists," Lester has observed, ". . . are struck by the haphazard variations in . . . rates and by the 'irrationality' of many intraplant and interplant differentials in wages."[4] The cents-per-hour result of negotiations will as often defy

---

[1] Sidney and Beatrice Webb, *Industrial Democracy* (2d ed.; London: Longmans, Green, 1920), p. 229.

[2] Fall River Textile Mfrs. Assn. and Textile Workers, 11 *LA* 988 (1949). For similar complaints concerning the state of wage theory, see Wilson Compton, "Wage Theories in Industrial Arbitration," *American Economic Review*, VI (July, 1916), 330; George Soule, "The Relation between Wages and National Productivity," *Annals of the American Academy of Political and Social Science*, C (March, 1922), 86; E. M. Patterson, "Factors Determining Real Wages," *Annals of the American Academy of Political and Social Science*, C (March, 1922), 83; Arthur M. Ross, *Trade Union Wage Policy* (Berkeley: University of California Press, 1948), pp. 1–2; Edwin E. Witte, "Criteria in Wage Rate Determinations," *Washington University Law Quarterly* (Fall, 1949), pp. 28–29.

[3] Quoted in Compton, *op. cit.*, p. 342.

[4] Richard A. Lester, "Wage Diversity and Its Theoretical Implications," *Review of Economic Statistics*, XXVIII (August, 1946), 152.

logic as comport with it. Hence the arbitrator—to strum an old string—must be as much artist as scientist, as frequently inconsistent as rigorous.

This brings us, again, to that most pervasive and influential of forces in wage determination, the comparison. Unlike other standards—cost of living, financial condition, substandards, productivity—this one requires neither logical analysis nor defense. There is no compulsion upon the arbitrator to look behind the adjustment in the comparison unit. The wage leader, in fact, may have had an entirely spurious basis for selecting the amount he chose. Here, however, eyebrows are not raised when sound conclusions are drawn from indefensible assumptions.

The force of the comparison is related to the basic and tough question of the effect of arbitration upon wages. Do wages rise more rapidly when they are arbitrated or when they are negotiated? Several interrelated factors suggest that the long-run result tends to be the same regardless of mechanics. The first, as noted, is the parity concept. The action of the wage leader spreads to the followers; the persuasiveness of his action is as great with the parties as it is with the neutral. A second factor, closely related to the first, is the antidifferential effect of collective wage determination. Economists have often observed that bargaining narrows or eliminates all forms of differentials—between employees in the same firm, between companies in the same industry, between industries, and between regions. Since wage arbitration is a phase of collective bargaining, it is proper to assume that it has the same equalizing effect. A third consideration is the moderating nature of arbitration. "Very few extreme settlements are made by arbitration boards," Oliver has declared. "The temporary factors which make other types of settlement so frequently reflect sudden changes in bargaining power have much less effect upon arbitration decisions."[5] Finally, the arbitrator works under the acceptability compulsion. With respect to wages, this means that he is influenced by the criteria that would have moved the parties and that the cents-per-hour result approximates what they would have agreed upon in his absence.

The conclusion, then, is that in general and in the long run there tends to be little difference in effect if wages are arbitrated rather than negotiated. This is the point to inject the caveat that an exceptional award may deviate from the rule.

The discussion of the impact of arbitration on wages has thus far been cast in generalities. A recent empirical study for the transit in-

---

[5] E. L. Oliver, "The Arbitration of Labor Disputes," *University of Pennsylvania Law Review*, LXXXIII (December, 1934), 222.

dustry supports the above conclusion.⁶ Kuhn's analysis merits summary at length. Before doing so, however, a point should be made about the subject matter of his study in relation to the present one. He was interested in only one industry—the one with the greatest experience with wage arbitration—but ours is more general. Further, the street railway union is noted for its skill and effectiveness in arbitrating. If it has done little better in arbitration than in negotiations, it is not unreasonable to assume that other labor organizations have not surpassed it and perhaps have not done as well.

Kuhn sought to measure the effect of arbitration upon transit wage changes with a variety of yardsticks. First, he found that all the arbitrated wage changes in this industry exceeded those reached by negotiations in the period of 1919–1948 by only 0.6 per cent. Second, taking a year of wage decline, 1921, he discovered that employees whose wages were arbitrated suffered an average reduction of 10.1 per cent, while those whose rates were negotiated lost 11 per cent. Third, examining a period of wage advance, 1946–1947, he found that the unweighted average of arbitrated increases was 15.5 per cent as compared with 13.3 per cent for the others. Fourth, the eleven firms with the highest incidence of arbitrated wages showed almost exactly the same average wage change as the whole industry over the thirty-year period. Finally, in comparing the long-run wage movement in transit with other industries, he discovered that transit had moved up less rapidly than manufacturing as a whole.

Kuhn's general conclusion for transit is as follows:

It may apparently be anticipated that a given wage decision selected at random in a given year will be higher if arbitrated than if not. On the other hand, there are no grounds to anticipate that the long-run wage level of individual firms will be higher, on the average, if they arbitrate regularly than if they do not. Nor is there any reason to believe that the average wage level of the industry has been raised as a result of arbitration. Arbitration in the transit industry apparently provides higher wages in particular, but not in general. . . .⁷

What is the significance of this conclusion for bargaining strategy with respect to arbitrating wages? It means, first, that the employer need seldom fear an award that is out of line on the high side and that the union has little reason to anticipate one that is unacceptably low. Second, the weak union or employer (association) may do a little better

⁶ Alfred Kuhn, *Arbitration in Transit, an Evaluation of Wage Criteria,* Labor Relations Series (Philadelphia: University of Pennsylvania Press, 1952), chap. 10.
⁷ *Ibid.,* p. 160. A comparison of wage trends in nations with compulsory arbitration and those without it produced much the same result. Australia and New Zealand, that is, have had a similar wage experience as nations that do not require arbitration by law. Carter Goodrich, "Arbitration, Industrial," *Encyclopedia of the Social Sciences,* XX (1930), 156.

for itself in the particular wage bargain by arbitrating. Conversely, if either is strong, it should normally avoid submitting wages to a neutral. Finally, the decision to arbitrate should be based not primarily upon the probable wage result but rather upon the prospects for a work stoppage. If the union cannot take a strike, it will do well to arbitrate and the employer not to arbitrate wages. If the union is prepared to shut the plant, both sides will find arbitration, costly as it is, much cheaper than a work stoppage.

This line of analysis suggests that collective bargaining and arbitration have differing potentialities in the wage area, that the range of the former is greater. Arbitration, in other words, is a more "conservative" process. As Hepburn has held:

An arbitrator cannot often justify an award involving the imposition of entirely novel relationships or responsibilities. These must come as a result of collective bargaining or through legislation. In rare cases, I concede it would be appropriate for an arbitrator to make an award entirely unique in an industry and area, as where conditions shock one's sense of equity and decency.
Nothing like that exists in this case, however.[8]

Arbitration, therefore, is not adapted to the wage leadership dispute. Hence sophisticated bargainers do not submit such cases and sometimes, as with the United Mine Workers, denounce the whole process of contract arbitration. Occasionally, however, a wage leader case does go to arbitration with unhappy results for the union.[9] The conclusion for bargaining is clear: the parties should recognize that wage arbitration has limitations that do not restrict negotiations. Arbitrators cannot grant some demands, and they should not be asked to do so.

Wage arbitration, too, is differentially effective with respect to the criteria of wage determination. That is, it can be more useful with standards based upon facts rather than upon conceptions and with those that are precisely translatable into cents per hour rather than those that are not. Parties who submit wages to arbitration, therefore, may expect more satisfactory results if their primary emphasis is upon comparisons and cost of living. They are more likely to be disappointed if they lay stress upon financial condition, differential features, substandards, and productivity. Here, again, unions and employers should not ask more of wage arbitration than it can give.

---

[8] Tampa Transit Lines and Amalgamated Street Railway Employees, 3 *LA* 196–197 (1946). See also Twin City Rapid Transit Co. and Amalgamated Street Railway Employees, 7 *LA* 845 (1947); California Grocers Assn. and Retail Clerks, 13 *LA* 245 (1949); Liquid Carbonic Corp. and Teamsters, 14 *LA* 655 (1950); United Press Assns. and Commercial Telegraphers, 14 *LA* 862 (1950); Note, "Factors Relied on by Arbitrators in Determining Wage Rates," *Columbia Law Review*, XLVII (September, 1947), 1032.

[9] Spear & Co. and Salesmen's Assn., 9 *LA* 567 (1948).

INDEX OF CASES CITED

INDEX OF CASES CITED

Aliquippa & Southern Railroad Co. and Railroad Workers, 16 *LA* 539 (1951), 61

American Fisheries Co. and Cannery Workers, 5 *LA* 220 (1946), 91

Art Chrome Co. and Furniture Workers, 11 *LA* 932 (1948), 82, 83

Associated General Contractors and Operating Engineers, 9 *LA* 201 (1947), 77, 100

Atlantic City Transportation Co. and Amalgamated Street Railway Employees, 9 *LA* 577 (1948), 6, 82, 84, 85, 86

Atlantic & Gulf Coast Shippers and Maritime Union, 4 *LA* 466 (1946), 57
—— 6 *LA* 700 (1947), 93
—— 9 *LA* 632 (1948), 37, 38

Auburn Shoe Mfrs. Assn. and Lewiston-Auburn Shoe Workers, 11 *LA* 594 (1948), 80, 82

Bates Mfg. Co. and Textile Workers, 18 *LA* 631 (1952), 45

Bay Cities Transit Co. and Amalgamated Street Railway Employees, 11 *LA* 747 (1948), 75, 83, 85

Beach Transit Corp. and Transport Workers, 11 *LA* 639 (1948), 79, 82

Beck, A. S., Shoe Corp. and Longshoremen and Warehousemen, 7 *LA* 924 (1947), 87

Berkshire Street Railway Co. and Amalgamated Street Railway Employees, 10 *LA* 133 (1948), 53

Birmingham Electric Co. and Amalgamated Street Railway Employees, 7 *LA* 673, 834 (1947), 81, 105

Blue Print Co. and Photographic Employees, 7 *LA* 154 (1947), 69

Boker, H., & Co. and Mine Workers, District 50, 12 *LA* 608 (1949), 38

Brockton Gas Light Co. and Utility Workers, 8 *LA* 124 (1947), 87

California Grocers Assn. and Retail Clerks, 13 *LA* 245 (1949), 67, 114

California Street Cable Railway Co. and Amalgamated Street Railway Employees, 7 *LA* 91 (1947), 81, 83, 93

Camburn and United Electrical Workers, 6 *LA* 636 (1947), 81

Capital Transit Co. and Amalgamated Street Railway Employees, 1 *LA* 204 (1946), 64

—— 9 *LA* 666 (1947), 6, 17–18, 40, 59, 62, 80, 82, 83, 84, 85, 86, 103

Champion Aero Metal Products and United Electrical Workers, 7 *LA* 278 (1947), 64, 82, 83, 84

Chesapeake & Potomac Telephone Co. and Maryland Fed. of Telephone Workers, 7 *LA* 630 (1947), 72

Cleveland Electric Illuminating Co. and Utility Workers, 8 *LA* 597 (1947), 68, 69

Columbia University and Transport Workers, 5 *LA* 311 (1946), 102

Committee for Tanker Cos. and Marine Engineers, 12 *LA* 855 (1949), 37, 57, 59, 62

Consolidated Edison System and Utility Workers, 6 *LA* 830 (1947), 69

Crawford Clothes and Retail, Wholesale and Department Store Employees, 5 *LA* 170 (1946), 63

Dairyland Power Coop. and Brotherhood of Electrical Workers, 4 *LA* 431 (1946), 64
—— 14 *LA* 737 (1950), 6, 59, 64, 83, 84

D. C. Trucking Assn. and Teamsters, 1 *LA* 89 (1946), 91

Detroit News and Brotherhood of Electrical Workers, 12 *LA* 1110 (1949), 91

Durso & Geelan Co. and Teamsters, 17 *LA* 748 (1951), 6

Employees' National Conference Committee and Eastern, Western and Southeastern Carriers' Conference Committees, 2 *LA* 286 (1946), 43

Employees Transit Lines and Amalgamated Street Railway Employees, 4 *LA* 748 (1946), 104

Fall River Textile Mfrs. Assn. and Textile Workers, 11 *LA* 984 (1949), 12, 37, 59, 67, 88, 111

Felters Co. and Textile Workers, 13 *LA* 702 (1949), 65

Fifth Ave. Coach Co. and Transport Workers, 4 *LA* 548 (1946), 57, 59, 67, 81

Four Milk Companies and Operating Engineers, 10 *LA* 470 (1948), 63

Full-Fashioned Hosiery Mfrs. and Hosiery Workers, 14 *LA* 321 (1950), 82

GENERAL INDEX

GENERAL INDEX